At trail's end no fertile valleys, no gold mines, no thriving ports are reached. The Pacific Crest Trail, like the other National Scenic Trails, is not a corridor to an economic end but rather is a process for individual change and growth. Although the trail's end is a desirable goal, it is not a necessary one, for the traveler is enriched in a nonmaterial sense with every step he takes along the way.

Jeffrey P. Schaffer
Drs. Bev & Fred Hartline
The Pacific Crest Trail, Volume 2

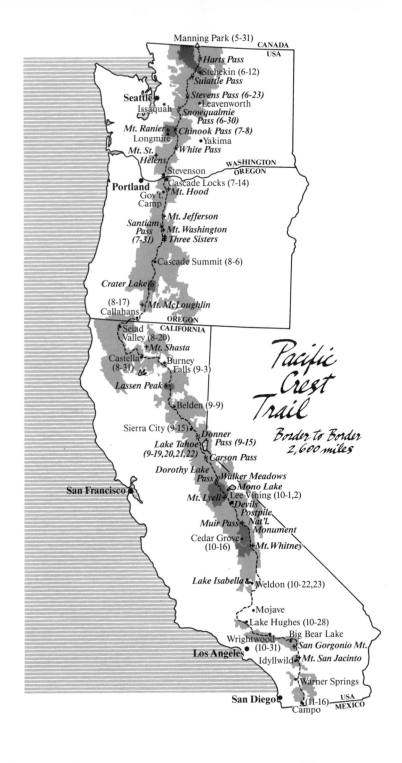

Manning Park (5-31)

CANADA
USA

Harts Pass
•Stehekin (6-12)
Suiattle Pass

Seattle
Issaquah
Stevens Pass (6-23)
•Leavenworth
Snowqualmie
Pass (6-30)
Mt. Ranier
Longmire
Chinook Pass (7-8)
•Yakima
Mt. St.
Helens
White Pass

Stevenson
WASHINGTON
OREGON
Cascade Locks (7-14)
Portland
Gov't.
Camp
Mt. Hood

Santiam
Mt. Jefferson
Pass
Mt. Washington
(7-31)
Three Sisters

•Cascade Summit (8-6)

Crater Lake

(8-17)
Callahans
Mt. McLoughlin

OREGON
CALIFORNIA
Seiad
Valley (8-20)
Mt. Shasta
Castella
•Burney
(8-31)
Falls (9-3)
Lassen Peak

•Belden (9-9)

Sierra City (9-15)
Donner
Pass (9-15)
Lake Tahoe
(9-19,20,21,22)
Carson Pass

Dorothy Lake
Pass
Walker Meadows
Mono Lake
San Francisco
Lee Vining (10-1,2)
Mt. Lyell
Devils
Postpile
Muir Pass
Nat'l.
Cedar Grove
Monument
(10-16)
Mt.Whitney

Lake Isabella
•Weldon (10-22,23)

•Mojave
•Lake Hughes (10-28)
Wrightwood
Big Bear Lake
(10-31)
San Gorgonio Mt.
Los Angeles
Idyllwild
Mt. San Jacinto

Warner Springs
San Diego
USA
(11-16)
MEXICO
Campo

Pacific
Crest
Trail

Border to Border
2,600 miles

SIX-MOON TRAIL

Canada to Mexico Along the Pacific Crest

by Tom Marshburn

edited by Robert K. Leishman

designed and illustrated
by Deborah Wilson Lord

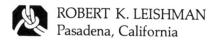 ROBERT K. LEISHMAN
Pasadena, California

International Standard Book Number 0-9614526-0-9

Library of Congress Catalog Card Number: 85-50297

Printed in the United States of America

Table of Contents

Illustrations

Illustrator/Designer

Deborah Wilson Lord grew up in Pasadena, California, with pencil in hand, encouraged by her artist (animator) father. Before taking up art as a career, she was a music major at Pasadena City College, where she marched with the band and played in both chamber orchestra and percussion ensemble. She also played for a while in a rock and roll band and was drummer for a college affiliated group called The Sandpipers.

In 1970, when she was nineteen, Debbie worked on a full-length feature film for Fine Arts Films, her father's company. Between 1971 and 1977, she worked in publication design, including an assignment as art director for a company that published "Pasadena Magazine." In 1977 she started her own graphic design company and did work for clients that included Walt Disney Educational Media. In 1979 she went to work full-time for Walt Disney Enterprises as a lead graphic designer for Epcot Center and Tokyo Disneyland. Debbie met Rudy Lord while working at Disney, and the couple honeymooned while both were on assignment in Tokyo.

For two wild weeks in the summer of 1971, Debbie took a solo motorcycle trip on a '71 BMW, traveling from Pasadena to Boston and back — a trip that included driving during a rainstorm at night while crossing the Rockies; a crash just outside Lincoln, Nebraska; sitting in for a drummer in a band playing at the Holiday Inn in Fremont, Nebraska; a high-speed race with a BMW car in Illinois; getting a ticket on the Pennsylvania Turnpike; and taking in the sights of St. Louis with friends. Out of money by the time she reached Amarillo, Texas, on her return trip, she spent the night on a concrete bench in a rest area there before driving nonstop back to Pasadena.

Debbie backpacked in the Sierra prior to her marriage to Rudy, and now they go into the mountains with sons Nathan and Christopher, both of whom prefer walking on a trail to stream fording and bushwacking. Before beginning the pencil illustrations that complement Tom's journal, she read his manuscript and studied photographs taken by Tom and his friends. She also made several Sierra backpack trips both to photograph specific scenes and to get the feel of being back on the trail.

Debbie had full design responsibility for *Six-Moon Trail,* including dust jacket and cover (headings and captions are her calligraphy). While it took Tom six months to complete his hike, it took Debbie two years to design and illustrate the book. Not only did she have an ongoing graphics arts practice to maintain, but she alone selected the subject matter for each illustration and insisted that the final result should depict the action both in technically correct detail and in the way experienced by Tom —a process that could be hurried only by making concessions that she was unwilling to accept.

Foreword

How can a book describe the psychological factors a person must prepare for . . . the despair, the alienation, the anxiety and especially the pain, both physical and mental, which slices to the very heart of the hiker's volition, which are the real things that must be planned for? No words can transmit those factors, which are more a part of planning than the elementary rituals of food, money, and equipment, and how to get them.

Pacific Crest Trail Hike Planning Guide,
edited by Chuck Long

When my hiking companion Rick and I first chanced upon Tom Marshburn, it was early in October, 1980, and there was a hint in the air of that fragile quality which John Muir was wont to describe in his writings as Indian summer. The sky was bright and fathomless, the air still and fragrant, and the meadow silent, as if poised for sleep. Lyell Fork of the Tuolumne meandered unhurriedly north, its reduced volume a clue of impending winter, and the two of us were striding purposefully south, towards our first campsite at the foot of Donohue Pass, eager to come within view of 13,157-foot Mt. Ritter which we hoped to climb two days hence. Tom was hiking in shorts, his legs noticeably thin, his pack ponderous, and his appearance mutely testifying to his months already on the trail. We might first have passed him as he rested alongside the creek bank, then he must have passed us during our lunch break, and finally we were walking together. He seemed relieved when we suggested that he join us in making camp well before the trail began its climb towards the pass, and at a wooded area suitable for spreading our bags, we halted for the day. Tom, I recall, mixed up a pot of gummy noodles in a battered aluminum container, while Rick and I began our meal with soup and ended it three courses later with cookies. After cleaning up camp and hanging our food bags, we gathered around the fire and visited until the Sierra worked its magic on us, our last sentences coming sleepily from the warmth and comfort of our bags.

The three of us started out on the trail together the next morning, but soon Tom lagged, as he labored under his immense pack, and not until the summit did we regroup. We walked some distance further after a brief rest, stopped later for lunch, then continued together for a short distance, parting abruptly as Rick and I struck off cross-country towards Mt. Ritter while Tom walked on in the direction of Emerald Lake. We had talked about getting together when Tom passed through the San Gabriel Mountains north of Los Angeles, but the weather turned stormy by mid-October, and Rick and I speculated that Tom had had to abort his hike.

Although Tom and I corresponded several times, not until more than two years had passed did we meet again, this time when I traveled to Charlottesville where he was in his first year of graduate school at the University of Virginia. The purpose of my trip was to talk with him about his journals — which I had understood when on the trail with him to be weather damaged and incomplete, but which he had recently described to me as reasonably whole — and while there I got swept up into what he refers to with characteristic understatement as the hike.

Hiking the complete Pacific Crest Trail has been referred to as the backpacking equivalent of scaling Mt. Everest, something that maybe 150 to 400 hikers have achieved within the last ten years.[1] The authors of the guide books that Tom carried reported that they were able to locate published evidence of the idea for such a trail as far back as 1926, but not until the 1960s, when backpacking began to appeal to large numbers of people, did the pioneering work done by Clinton C. Clarke of Pasadena, who is generally credited with the concept of a Pacific Crest Trail, and Warren L. Rogers, who led the exploration activities, begin to materialize. In 1968, through enactment of the National Trails System Act, Congress set the framework for a system of trails and specifically made the Appalachian and the Pacific Crest trails the first two National Scenic Trails.[2]

The approximately 2,600-mile long Pacific Crest Trail doesn't always follow the crest, nor is it always a trail.[3] In 1971 the Forest Service published a guide which stipulated that the trail should stay close to the crest and that its grade should not exceed a fifteen-foot rise for one hundred horizontal feet; and while it is usually a trail, sometimes it is a road, but rarely is it true cross-country travel. It is not a "center line" that can be "precisely and unambiguously followed"; rather, "it is only a route."[4]

Trail history, hike planning, natural history, and trail guide information have all been included in *The Pacific Crest Trail,* guide books published by Wilderness Press of Berkeley, California, and the authors (Jeffrey P. Schaffer, Ben Schifrin, Thomas Winnett, and J. C. Jenkins for Volume One; Jeffrey P. Schaffer and Drs. Bev and Fred Hartline for Volume Two) share the achievement of making the hike possible.

Tom Marshburn turned twenty while on the trail in 1980. He had first begun thinking about the hike in 1975, but not until 1978, while hiking in the Appalachians and experiencing the discomfort of storm conditions, did he conclude that he could handle the Pacific Crest. Somewhat incongruously, however, when he finally decided to do it, he had only one month for the actual preparations.

Tom had completed his sophomore year at Davidson College in North Carolina when he began the hike. Because he could not arrive at the trailhead much before June first, he was forced to begin in Canada, rather than to make the typical Mexico to Canada trek. Otherwise, he would have faced Washington in November and winter conditions that he was unprepared for. The guide books are written south to north, so Tom began reading at the back of volume two and worked his way backwards over topographic maps and through text until he finished volume one. It is understandable when on the trail somewhere in California he gets confused as to which direction he should be walking and is straightened out by an obliging trail maintenance worker.

Atlanta, Georgia, is home to Tom. His father is a Presbyterian minister there, his mother a homemaker. The youngest member in a family that includes three brothers and three sisters, Tom found one of the most difficult aspects of the hike being far from home, family, and friends. At Davidson College he majored in physics, and in December of 1983, he was concluding his first year of graduate work in physics and engineering at the University of Virginia at Charlottesville. Tom's three brothers and one of his sisters are medical doctors; one of his two remaining sisters is a physical therapist and the other a nurse. His choice of masters thesis subject — biomedical engineering — suggests that he too might be leaning in the direction of a medically related career. A continuing love is art, and as a youngster he outlined and wrote mystery stories as well as did some painting with acrylics. Jules Verne was a favorite author of his in those days, and adventure travel was a favorite genre. During visits to the farm of his paternal grandparents, Tom developed a love of the wild that was rekindled on the trail. His parents, Granny Marshburn, and his brothers — the latter whom he admires for their passionate interest in science and their equally strong love of people — are all persons whose influence upon him has been profound.

Food became so appreciated during the hike that after he returned home, Tom found that he could no longer leave the table with any food still on his plate. He also learned to enjoy camping without a fire, and he got so that the further he hiked, the more pride he took in packing out his litter. His introduction to technical climbing on Mt. Ranier heightened his interest in mountaineering, and while at the University of Virginia, he served with an active mountain rescue unit.

Reading while on the hike provided essential mental stimulation and took Tom's mind off the rigors of the trail, his books more than justifying their considerable weight. June in Washington was too wet for much reading, but later he read by firelight and while walking, completing one book while crossing the Mojave Desert (a possible explanation for why he failed to see any rattlers!). He had taken up the classical guitar in 1979 and on occasion wished that he had the instrument with him; but he had to content himself with harmonica and voice. The most difficult lesson for him to learn and practice was to take one day at a time. Tom does not contemplate more long distance hiking, although he would like sometime to climb Mt. McKinley.

The trip cost Tom $2,300.00 in money he had saved, most of which went for food. Air fare, postage, and film related costs were the other major expense categories. Tom carried very little freeze dried food because of the relatively high cost — just enough to tide him through the stormiest nights. He did consume vitamins, powdered protein, dense foods, and lots of carbohydrates. His favorite items were peanut butter, noodles (with a variety of flavorings), and nuts. He craved dairy products, fruits, vegetables, breads, and pastries. The dry foods he carried double wrapped in plastic bags, weight being a major consideration. He packed and daily referred to the guide book, *The Pacific Crest Trail* (Volume 1 in California; Volume 2 in Washington and Oregon; the second and third editions, respectively); and although he did carry a compass, he did not feel that it was needed. Major items of equipment that he took included a Svea stove, a fiber filled sleeping bag (down he considered virtually useless when wet), gaiters, crampons, and a lightweight trail boot with Vibram sole called Vasque Cascade, which served him well. His ice ax was lost at Mt. Hood, Oregon, his tent in California near Castella. He missed the ax, which was useful as a tool and walking stick, besides being an essential item of safety equipment, but except for a few stretches of trail a hundred yards long or so in the Sierra, ice was not a problem during the remainder of the trip. (He is quick to concede that he should have practiced ice ax arrest before setting out on the hike.) The tent loss was severe, not entirely compensated for by the subsequent purchase of a tarp, but no tent would have overcome the affects of the mid October storm that was moving in on Tom as he hurried along the trail in the central Sierra.

In the Cascades, Tom and his party were unsure of just where they were much of the time, snow covering the ground and visibility often reduced to a few yards. Drowning, he heard, was the major cause of life loss in the mountains of Washington, and he got so that he would cross the streams with his boots on, preferring the discomfort that followed to the unsure footing of crossing barefoot and the loss of time involved in repeatedly removing and replacing foot gear. In an environment where injury was a daily threat and sickness a distinct possibility, Tom recognized that his blisters, recurring diarrhea, and occasional upset stomach — though more than mere irritations — were relatively minor afflictions. A few times he chided himself for lack of coordination, but he was probably overly critical. One turns one's ankle or slips on a stair tread or damp walk and thinks nothing of it at home, while a similar occurrence along a narrow ledge with fifteen hundred feet of sheer drop is difficult to ignore. But as real as were the risks of injury — even fatality, or of sickness, these paled when compared with an entirely different sort of challenge — one that can best be communicated in Tom's own words as we join him on the hike.

Notes to Foreword

1. "It is unknown how many people completed the entire hike — an achievement comparable in backpacking to scaling Mt. Everest." "Pacific Crest Trail — A 2,606-Mile Odyssey Through Wilderness" by Allan Parachini. Published October 30, 1983. Copyright, 1983, *Los Angeles Times.* Reprinted by permission.

2. Jeffrey P. Schaffer and Bev and Fred Hartline, *The Pacific Crest Trail,* Vol. 2 (Wilderness Press, 1979), 1-3.

3. Jeffrey P. Schaffer, Ben Schifrin, Thomas Winnett, and J. C. Jenkins, *The Pacific Crest Trail,* Vol. 1 (Wilderness Press, 1982), 5 and 38.

4. Jeffrey P. Schaffer and Bev and Fred Hartline, Op. Cit., 3-6.

Editing Notes

Tom Marshburn made his journal entries during the hike, filling four slender, spiral bound notebooks. Snow and rain rendered some pages in the first notebook difficult to read, but he was able to rewrite these entries exactly as he originally wrote them.

There were a few places in the journals where entries were missing, and Tom has filled these gaps from his recollections, which are understandably still vivid. He may have neglected to finish an entry, or thought he made an entry when he had not, or he may have inadvertently destroyed a page when he tore out paper for letter writing purposes. On one particular occasion, he intentionally removed and destroyed an entry. But in every instance, the missing material has been noted and a summary given of what took place. In this sense, then, the journals provide an unbroken record of Tom's thoughts and experiences during the hike.

In addition to filling in the gaps, editing the text included double checking place names, correcting less than a handful of wrong names, correcting spelling and punctuation, and making a few improvements in syntax. Occasionally a word or phrase was changed or even eliminated, usually to lessen redundancy. Left in place were a few words not commonly found in dictionaries, such as gruffing, spritzed, and grungy. Their meaning will be clear from context. Where a sentence is left incomplete, this is how Tom wrote it to express his thought or convey a feeling.

Tom's book is not intended as a trail guide, but it is possible to match place names with guide book descriptions and maps, and to follow him in considerable detail as he makes his way along the Pacific Crest from Canada to Mexico — and this is precisely what was done during the editing.

*"It shot straight out of the clouds
like a castle."*

Manning Park to Cascade Locks

I should like to ask the assessors what is the value of that blue mountain range in the northwest horizon to Concord, and see if they would laugh or seriously set about calculating it . . . . If I were one of the fathers of the town I would not sell this right which we now enjoy for all the merely material wealth and prosperity conceivable. If need were, we would rather all go down together.

Henry David Thoreau
The Journal of Henry D. Thoreau

May 30

I was wondering if I'd be able to see Mt. Rainier. A flat carpet of clouds lay below the plane, and I craned my neck to catch a glimpse of the Cascades below them. Intermittent breaks in the cloud cover revealed views that really worked their magic on me. Snow lay matted on the peaks and gutted the valleys. There were sharp ridges. I felt like I had been moved to December. It was kind of sad, very much like a dream, because I really did feel like I was back in winter. The pilot's voice: "You can see Mt. Rainier to your left...." I strained my eyes and thought I saw a peak sticking up above the cloud cover. It didn't seem that big; then I looked to my right. There it was. I couldn't believe it. Although we flew high over these miniature crests and valleys, we wouldn't have even cleared Rainier. I couldn't help saying "Oh, God" over and over again. It shot straight out of the clouds like a castle. It was beautiful. I'll never forget it. We'll have to try to climb that thing. It was completely caked with white, shimmering ice.

June 5

Here I am, six days later and no entries. Well, the past days have gone by in one big blur — days I'll remember with relish, but only because man has the ability to forget the bad and retain the good. The plane landed at a cloud-covered Seattle, and for an hour I walked around the ultra-modern Seattle airport trying to convince myself that I was really on the west coast. A small jet flown by two guys wearing turbans took me to Vancouver. I was so dead tired of going through customs that I was trying to take off my pack, but just as I sat on the conveyor belt, some guy flipped the switch. A customs officer grabbed me before I got squeezed onto the luggage rack. Tommy at his best. Then, leaving Vancouver, a really nice guy offered to give me a ride to a bus stop. It was two in the morning. Talking about Mt. St. Helens volcano, I asked if he had seen any ash, and he said, "No man, I don't even do any marijuana." I didn't say anything else. For the next hour I rode around on trolley buses, the only passenger, until finally I got to a place where I could walk to meet Bob. There he was, in front of the Greyhound bus station. Both dead tired, we checked into the Alkazar Hotel at three in the morning. Kind of funny: here we were in Canada, and this hotel had a Mexican decor. Kind of symbolic, too. The next day, second thoughts about the trip really burdened me. Mom had put a note in my pants (which I've had in my shirt pocket since), and I just began to really miss home;[1] and I also began wondering whether Bob and I would get along. Our personalities are so different; I felt like I'd dumped a wad of money into something that was going to be a nightmare. I also felt like I was dumping Mom and Dad with a lot of things. It really depressed me. I felt like an irresponsible outcast.

The mountains do something to you, though. After driving four hours from Vancouver to Manning Park on a bus, I felt better. I had talked the whole time with a twenty-seven-year-old Canadian girl named Sonja and glanced periodically at some stupendous mountains. We finally arrived at 11:00 P.M., and Bob and I left a bus full of sleeping people and stepped into the perfectly silent, dark, and rain-drenched Manning Park Lodge. How weird to finally be at a place I had seen so many pictures of, and how many happy PCT hikers had finished their journey here. Bob and I slept behind the lodge in my tent next to some tennis courts. Next morning was beautiful. We asked a red-haired lady at the hotel desk for wilderness permits. Her answer was a heavy blow; it hit like an anvil. "No, you can't go out there. People always swear they'll be able to hike out, and we have to go look for them by helicopter. It's impossible until July 15. No one has ever made it before. If we could stop you, we would."

Bob and I talked it over. We couldn't travel across the country and just not go. The ranger there asked if we had had a lot of experience. I said "Yes," with a slight tinge of a lie hanging on the end. He gave us the permits. While Bob and I were having our last meal of French toast and pancakes at the restaurant, some guy walked up whom I had never seen before and asked, "You guys still going on the PCT?" I said, "Yes." He said, "Good luck, you're going to need it." Bob and I were real antsy before we left. A cloud cover rolled in as we looked for the beginning of the trail off the highway. Little did we know how much we were to hate those clouds later.

What a relief! We met three hikers — Bill, Katy, and Penny, who were leaving the day after us to hike the thing. At least we knew we had some partners who were crazy enough to try this now. This whole thing was turning into an adventure story. We were scared. Well, at 12:55 P.M. Bob and I put our first step on the PCT. The sky was still overcast and, as a slight drizzle was falling, we could look down and see Manning Park as we climbed Windy Joe Mountain. There were patches of snow here and there. Bob loved the snow. We crossed over Windy Joe and could see our first snowcapped mountain. Clouds enveloped the top of that. Tree frogs garrumphed in the valley below.[2] We thought it was a bear at first.

I wish I could put more of my feelings down rather than just what happened, but looking back I can't blame myself for not writing then. That morning in Manning Park was the last time we were to see blue sky for what seemed like an eternity.

Bob and I camped after only a six-mile hike. We had lots of food. The next morning, after a quick breakfast and tooth brushing, we were hiking across Castle Creek, and then at the U.S.-Canadian border at Monument 78. Again, I couldn't believe that I was there. I had seen so many pictures of this miniature Washington Monument made of brass that I had to keep telling myself over and over that I was near the west coast, near Washington, over three thousand miles away from home. We could see the towering, jagged points of Castle Crags, swept with snow. Constantly at our ears was a far-away whooshing sound, like a distant river or wind. Otherwise, it was silent.

Our first mile in the U.S. brought several views of magnificent snow-caked mountains, but clouds constantly covered up the highest peaks. Bob and I were taking it too easy; Bill, Katy, and Penny passed us. We finally hit a snowfield about forty feet wide. Walking over it wasn't difficult until I punched through into a cavity below the snow. Bob helped me out. How many more times that was going to happen!

The drizzle turned into a light snow. We hiked past an avalanche slope where two ice boulders, a deep blue color, had rolled to the bottom. We finally began climbing to Castle Pass, and the snow was about ankle deep. We caught up with the group of three ahead of us and, after a brief snowball fight, continued on.

We had only known these three for about twenty minutes, and yet already I felt like I had known them all my life. Backpacking does that to people; both fears and pleasures bring a common bond. The hike to Hopkins Pass was very tiring. We crossed two 45° slopes, lost the trail, and ended up having to enter Hopkins Pass down a steep rocky slope. I slipped once, picked up speed quickly before I could orient my ice axe, and wrapped around a tree. No harm done. The clouds descended as we camped there at Hopkins Pass.

That was Sunday, June the first. As I said before, the next week was a blur. Those clouds never left us; we could only see for about a one hundred-foot radius around us. I'll never forget slogging through the knee-deep snow all day long, with the constant crunch of the ice axes as we had to plunge them into the snow with every step. All the hiking was on very steep slopes. The slope would come careening down from a cloud-covered summit and disappear at a harrowing angle below into the cloud-covered valley. All one could see was an extremely tilted slope with trees periodically. White-out conditions all the time; no horizon could be seen.

Lord, how can I describe how frustrating it is to punch thigh deep into the snow — the strain on one leg to lift up your body and fifty pound pack, and then to have that leg punch through too. This process was repeated hundreds of times every day. It was like going up steps without getting anywhere. All one could do was lay his forehead on his ice axe, regain composure and breath, and then keep going.

The cuss word became the major form of communication these days. I felt guilty about it, but it seemed to be an excellent way to deal with this type of hiking. Bob lets his words fly freely. Usually his first words of the morning are "goddamn, fuck." And he says it with great emphasis. This gets on my nerves some, but that's Bob.

"It was like going up steps without getting anywhere."

Even with clouds, though, the sun did its work on us. Reflecting off the snow, it burns the face, chin, nostrils. Lips become sandpaper. Those without sun goggles got a red streak straight across the middle of their eyeballs — a mild case of snow-blindness.

It sounds terrible writing about these bad things, but how can one describe the frustration of every morning waking up to clouds and snow — everything soaking wet and cold, not being able to sleep because you're shivering so hard, not being able to walk anywhere without slipping? Every single day it has snowed heavily on us, so that it is now five to eight feet deep. It wouldn't be so bad if at least we could see something, but all day every day we are encased in a box of fog. No views anywhere. Nothing, nothing at all, is dry. The only way to stay warm is hike.

On Powder Mountain, a couple of sunballs[3] rolled by two feet in front of me; and at Tamarack Peak, a large sheet of snow slid down the slope just where we had passed. I slipped a couple of times and was able to arrest myself all right. Once both feet punched through at the same time in a split position, and Bob had to come over and pull me out. One morning I fell through about five feet and slightly sprained my right ankle. It's still a little swollen.

The only way to find the trail is to hike in a straight line. Every hundred yards or so we find a tiny exposed patch of trail, about one by two feet. The switchbacks and passes are where we get lost. Then we split up and search; one sees four ghostly figures weaving around in the fog on the slope. Very eerie. Just look for a cut tree or bush, and usually that's the trail. A bit of detective work. It's very satisfying to hike a trail that you can only see every once in a while. Feel like an early pioneer or something.

I must admit, on Powder Mountain the clouds did lift for about twenty minutes. We saw a beautiful, dark green valley below, and grassy slopes. No grass up here at 6,500 feet. But then the clouds descended again. The valleys here are like bowls, very gradual and evenly sloped. The trees are beautiful — perfect cones, very tall and straight, and almost blue-green. A little wildlife: two grouse, one squirrel, and tree frogs. How a frog can live up here I don't know.[4]

All five of us hiked together this past week. Bill is an excellent pathfinder. He's tall with short blond hair and has a voice that sounds like he's trying to talk and hold his breath at the same time.

Here's an itinerary:
May 31 — Manning Park to Castle Creek Valley;
June 1 — to Hopkins Lake (camped in snow);
June 2 — to Woody Pass (camped in three feet of powder);
June 3 — to Holman Pass (snowed again);

June 4 — to Jim Pass (snowed again);
June 5 — to Windy Pass (still snowing).

And here, at Windy Pass, we found an abandoned mining cabin. It was locked, but we were too cold, wet, and hungry to feel guilty about breaking in. We got through the window. Oh, heaven! Two barrel shaped homemade stoves, some year-old ketchup, noodles, and salt. And two mattresses!

June 6

Here I am, Friday morning (June 6), writing this journal. We started to hike out after drying our equipment next to the stoves, but the noodles and ketchup and the blizzard outside made us decide to stay for the day. Ah, to be warm and dry — what a luxury! Our feet are all swollen from being cold so long. I just remembered how all five of us tried to sleep in a two-man tent at Holman Pass, so we could stay warm that night. Didn't work. And now we are just sitting around pouring over maps and writing in our journals.

Our partners are out of food, so they'll have to leave the trail and hitchhike to a town tomorrow. They miscalculated like crazy. Then it's just Bob and I for the second half of the hike to Stehekin. I wish I had a guitar.

Our first bit of blue sky. At about seven tonight the clouds began to move, and we saw a glorious sunset with orange alpenglow. The peaks are blue and white. They look like shattered blue glass. The ridge rolls away with sharp jagged mountains; first time we've seen them. Looks like the vast backbone of some gigantic ancient dinosaur. Blue sky. I hope it's still that way next morning. This morning we woke up in the cabin to the worst snowstorm yet. We all looked at each other and decided to eat the year-old macaroni on the shelves and stay another day. The macaroni tasted terrible, but once down it filled the stomach with a warm lump. I'm starting to dream about food. It's become an obsession. The sky is still a bright, electric blue, and it's after 10 P.M.

June 7

I haven't been keeping up like I should, so let me start where I left off. What an unbelievable four days this has been. I'll never forget them. We sorrowfully (wistfully is a better word) left the cabin the morning of June 7 and began our snow march again. For the first time the clouds had lifted, and one could see a breathtaking panorama of blue and white mountains. As we would round a slope, I could look into a valley and see three thousand feet down into bowl shaped, blue-green valleys. From each one came the roar of its own river. And the bear tracks! They're huge! About eight inches wide. Anyway, the snow fell again and again; our view left us. We punched through deeper and deeper until finally we hit a road, a jeep road leading to Hart's Pass. Because Bill, Penny, and Katy had so grossly miscalculated their food, they were going to hitchhike to Winthrop to get more food.

We plunged into Hart's Pass to see a locked guard station and a road with snow shoveled up fifteen feet on either side. Also visible — a pickup truck. A couple named Dave and Laurie — young, kind of English-looking — had been camping there and offered to drive the three down to Winthrop. Also, Dave gave Bob and myself a large Tupperware bowl full of spaghetti. I must have looked funny, considering how reverently I held that bowl. We said goodbye to the three as they drove off in the pickup. Bob and I were alone again, and we ate a meager lunch by the road. A chipmunk came within two feet of me to grab some peanuts that had fallen out of my gorp.[5] Man, those animals are fast. They just flicker from place to place.

Bob and I began following an old jeep road to hit the trail again, and we almost got lost. I really wonder how Bob and I will get along without the other three to distract us from each other. Katy had made an observation; she said Bob was more determined than I, and I am more patient than he. This really seemed to be true, because on the jeep road Bob began to get angry. He would slog in one direction, say, "Hell, that's not it," and turn around. I would walk a few steps further and see a sign. This happened two consecutive times during those two miles. But Bob sure can lead through the snow. When I'm tired and give up looking for the trail, he keeps on going and going.

We found a spot out of the snow during a short rain shower, and a high wind picked up, flapping the fly on our tent like crazy. We feasted on the spaghetti, wishing we had three times as much. Just before we went to bed, Bill, Katy, and Penny showed up. That guy Dave was so nice he had driven them down to town and all the way back again. Later, talking to Penny, I found out that Dave and Laurie were planning on getting married this November.

June 8

Today found us lost again. I was totally frustrated. The guidebook[6] had fallen out of my sweater five hundred feet down the slope. I went to get it, went into a slide, and wrapped around a tree upside down. The guidebook with all the maps was nearly ruined. I slipped in the snow several times more until I finally reached our footprints. By then the three had caught up. To find the trail, we climbed an avalanche chute to the top of the ridge. I don't know when I've been so scared. My heart was going ninety miles an hour. Rock climbing and ice climbing can be really frightening with a fifty-pound pack. The view at the top, however, was gorgeous. The peaks looked as if they had been shot from the center of the earth and had been frozen just as they were leaving the surface. We found the trail, even followed mountain goat tracks for awhile. Right before our destination, Glacier Pass, we stopped to glance at a map. In the five seconds we lowered our heads to the map and up again, a dense fog had squeezed through the pass and obscured everything. Then the sleet hit. We made a rapid retreat, jumped in our wet tents, ate supper while in the sleeping bags, and by the time we were about to go to sleep the sky had cleared up.

Nature seems many times out here to be just a pestering child, doing all it can to give you a hard time and mocking you. It almost develops an evil personality. But the might and majesty of these jagged peaks make you realize nature only does what it will, that you are a visitor, and in order to stay here you must accept any onslaught it may mindlessly give.

June 9

A beautiful morning — almost clear sky. We're on an ice-hard shimmering ridge with glistening peaks around. Feel on top of the world. Bob and I get an early start on a treacherous slope that climbs about twelve hundred feet: it's 45° and covered with a sheet of ice. I slipped on it and slid into the only rock around us. Funny, but then it didn't seem like a big deal. I broke a sapling when I hit the rock, and very fragrant pine scent came out. We decided to don our crampons.[7] We got lost by the time the three caught up but finally found the trail into Glacier Pass. We kept descending and finally met clear trail with no snow. It's amazing how much one notices the smell of the earth and green plants after being in the snow for so long. Different smells kept dazzling my nose. We tromped about two miles to a bridge, where we had lunch (lemon pudding), and the rest of the day we followed the river. Snow again, but a dry spot to sleep was found. First day of no precipitation. Camp was fun. We had a fire and some great puffball mushrooms and hot Jell-O, and Bill pulled out some popcorn.

June 10

Eleven-mile hike. We got lost on the way to Methow Pass. Everyone was so depleted from meager meals, we had a hard time even caring about finding the trail. An uphill climb in the snow brought us to the pass. Beautiful view, a great place for lunch. This has become my favorite time of day. There's no cooking, no fuss, just eating and admiring the view. For some reason a time like this makes all that work worthwhile. We could see clearly a line as the trail traversed the ridge. This was tough; my feet hurt. Back into deep snow. The trail just kept going up, up, until it circled a peak just below the summit. This part was shaky. Snow was piled on the trail, forming a wedge against the rock face of the mountain. We had to teeter on this knife edge with a straight five hundred-foot drop below us. Really scary. Cutthroat Pass was amazing — just snow and ice and the jagged summits of several peaks almost at eye level. I thought I was on another planet. But we plunged out of all that, down to a dry switchback, about two miles farther. No precipitation again.

Several changes have come over myself and all of us. For some reason, we all sing Christmas carols in our heads. I guess our fondest memories of home and the sight of snow do this to us. Everyone's biggest preoccupation is food. Food. The most elaborate, luscious, and even the simplest meals constantly plague our thoughts. I always think of food. I think of how much a luxury it is to eat when you want to at home. Several times I've gone through every detail of getting in my car, turning the ignition, going through every step of driving to buy a dozen doughnuts. Man! What I wouldn't give! These times I miss home the most. Every minute of time I can think of spent at home or Davidson[8] seems like heaven. I miss home so much. Every person, minute of relaxation, especially the food. I really wonder if I want to live six months like this without civilized, familiar surroundings. I still feel irresponsible being here. It really bothers me. Maybe things will change.

Everyone also has very vivid dreams. My dreams have been very sex-centered, but it's funny: when food is so important, thoughts of girls are very, very minimal. I haven't thought of them in awhile. I really don't care.

One interesting physiological change is that when my body wants to defecate, I have no choice. It just comes. All I can do is take off my pack and run off the trail. Oh well.

June 11-18

I forgot, back at Methow Pass we saw where a bear had taken a running slide down a chute. Lots of big pawprints and a long slash in the snow.

It's now June 19 as I write this. I'm tired of being behind in this thing; I forget so much I want to write, so I'll just highlight up to the present date.

June 7 — Windy Pass to just past Hart's Pass;
June 8 — to just before Glacier Pass;
June 9 — to camp beside Brush Creek;
June 10 — across Methow, Granite, and Cutthroat passes;
June 11 — to Hide-Away Camp, past Rainy Pass;
June 12 — to Stehekin;
June 13 — to Swamp Creek Camp;
June 14 — to near Suiattle Pass;
June 15 — to Suiattle River;
June 16 — to Dolly Vista;
June 17 — to Milk Creek;
June 18 — to five miles past Fire Creek Pass;
June 19 — to Kennedy Hot Springs.

The closer we got to Stehekin, the more homesick I got. Dreams of home are so vivid. Every moment there is now so precious and heaven-like. Getting to our first food drop makes me think of when I'll finish the trail and go home. What a joy. I even cried a little in the tent.

It was fun watching the three get their food cache. It was just like Christmas seeing how excited they were to pull out twelve more days of food. Bob and I went ahead. We got a little rain.

The next day we arrived at the dirt road to wait for the shuttle bus. We met Craig and John. The ride to Stehekin was great. To be moving without walking! One part of the road had a waterfall two inches from the left side of the bus and a drop-off two inches on the right. Neat ride.

Upon entering Stehekin, Bob and I jumped into the only cafe. What a luxurious dinner! I'll never forget it. We each had a salad; I had two and a half huge bowls of stew with one and a half servings of cornbread and two scoops of ice cream. A mistake. I was about to get sick, eating like that after shrinking my stomach for two weeks. John and Craig just sat next to us, chatting away.

John is thirtyish, has black stringy hair and beard, yellow crooked teeth. He works in an orchard for a season, picking, thinning, or pruning until he's made enough money to hike for a couple months. Very, very congenial. A great guy. Seems like he'll live forever.

The town is unbelievable. About forty people live here. A one-room schoolhouse, sixteen students, grades one through eight, and one teacher. Most homes are made by their owners from trees cut in the forest. One guy has a garden and goats and sells goat's milk cheese. His wife is famous for her bread (that was her cornbread I ate — fantastic). The store is the size of a bedroom.

Bob and I had pie and ice cream the next morning before we picked up our food and left. Goodbye, Stehekin! We will miss you!

The packs are full and heavy again, and surprisingly we see the three go tromping by as we are ready to leave. The last time I saw John he had his face to the sun and was hiking up McGregor Mountain.

The feet hurt badly. I jammed both big toes and am hobbling

along. Before long we hit our low campsite in the forest where water is plentiful and the wood burns quickly and fine. A nice fire. Bob and I drool as the three have cake for dinner and pancakes the next morning. Food is such a primary need now. We think of it constantly.

The next day's hike sent us up to the snow and, just like old times, I began punching through a lot. It's so frustrating, but I have to learn to keep my temper. A constant rain drove us to sleep in the snow. We're wet and cold.

The next day, the hike up to Suiattle Pass was maddening. Constantly up, up, up. But as always, the climb was worth it. Crossing a pass is an experience. One gets the best view of where he's been, and a whole new valley of where he's going opens up. The dull roar of a new river also hits you instantly as you come over the pass. It's very beautiful and fulfilling.

We got lost big time on the way down, but the promise of a low, dry campsite drove us on eight more miles. I really sank into my thoughts then; after food I think about what I'm going to do when I finish this hike. I really wonder if I'll finish this thing with all I'm going through psychologically, but I hope it's just a stage every hiker goes through.

Next day, a short hike up to snow again. We decide to camp early in a dry clump of trees surrounded by snow. Lots of rain, but heavy boughs on the trees above make for a nice evening.

The next morning is foggy and drizzly. We can hardly see and lose the trail for almost three hours in the snow. I just can't get motivated. I slog for a few steps, stop, slog, stop. We find the trail, eat lunch, and then make time to another low, but not very good, campsite. The clouds are low. Along the way we saw a newborn fawn, spots and all! on a switchback. We crashed through the woods well around it so as not to leave any human smell.

The next day (June 18) will always be in my memory. We climbed over a thousand feet to a snow mounded slope and eventually came to Mica Lake, frozen year-round. All around us was snow and ice and only ice-gripped mountains on the horizon. Eerily beautiful. We climbed above the lake, an exhausting segment, because we had to kick-step the whole way. Like climbing a steep staircase. After Fire Creek Pass, we descended through deep slush, then back up again. Tommy at his best — he keeps falling and sliding. My feet just don't belong to me. They do as they will. We traversed a basin and got lost again. Kennedy Hot Springs was our goal, but it was quickly slipping away. Katy was exhausted: she just sat and began crying. We traverse another bowl as clouds above Glacier Peak descend and force us to make camp on a ledge. I'm so exhausted I can't do anything at all. It's cold up here but somewhat dry. I went ahead and ate what I was planning to save for Kennedy. Everyone is quiet — spirits are low, we're just so hungry and depleted.

June 19

A blazing blue morning. The sky is electric blue, and the snow is bright white. Hurts the eyes. Everyone's kind of quiet; we just want to get to the hot springs.

How many guys can say they've sat in a hot springs with four other nude people, two of them girls? It's amazing how natural it seems out here. We've all been through a lot together, and it didn't bother them or me or anyone. Other hikers were around (this place is low and popular; no snow), and people didn't care if they had clothes on or not. Kind of neat, but totally unerotic. It just seemed like that's how it should be. The hot springs felt great. I hate to say this, but my first close brush with a bath in eighteen days. Once you arrive at a certain level of grossness, you just don't care anymore. My hair still isn't washed. It probably did more harm than good, for wiping off the oils on my skin really exposed it to future strong winds and made it dry and easily burned. But any chance I get I'm going to take a shower with soap.

It was a lazy day. We stopped hiking at eleven and set up camp. I just caught up in my journal and relaxed. We all needed it after the hard day before at Fire Creek Pass. After dinner that night, the three pulled out makings for s'mores! What a great dessert! And what a sacrifice they made to give that to us. It was good but really just whetted the appetite and made us want more.

Another hiker came by the campsite that night and told us they have brought back the register for the draft. This really depressed me. If the draft itself were reinstated, how could I hike around out here knowing I may have to leave home for a year? Going home seemed like heaven, but I'd almost made it through the hardest part. I got especially down when this guy began arguing with me whether I should go or not when I said I would go if drafted. I just went to bed.

Most hikers of any long-distance trail don't really figure out why they're doing it until later in the hike. This is my case. Sitting in the hot springs and talking to others helped me pick up another glimpse of why I'm here. One guy said, "That's great. It's one of those things, like running a marathon, that I want to do but know I never will."I guess one reason I'm here is so I won't have to say that. But man, do I miss home. More than ever before in my life.

June 20

Leaving the springs and the warm, low elevation was difficult, but we made excellent progress all the way to White Pass. About eight miles of no snow, which was nice. One portion of the trail opened onto a wide, bushy glade, and the sight and smell immediately made me think of the farm.[9] I knew then that although the west was beautiful, the east would forever hold my heart.

This was Bob's toughest day. Lunches are very sparse now. I had a can of tuna, about twice what anyone else had. After lunch, when we stopped to put on gaiters (more snow), Bob just couldn't get up. He sat there silently with his forehead in his hands. We still made fairly good time, however. Red Pass was gorgeous. Straight up a wall of snow we climbed, to get through a fifteen hundred-foot high ridge. Again, as at all passes, a whole new world opened up as I stepped up to the pass. Roars of new rivers suddenly met my ears, and a blast of wind hit my face. A whole new panorama, and we could see the trail as it traversed the ridge to White Pass, our camp for the night. What a good feeling to know your destination is near. Bill dropped his pack and picked up a few rocks when he saw a couple of grouse. Katy just laughed and sat down when he went tiptoeing over these steep slopes while the pudgy bird cruised along on its feet just out of reach. He hit a couple, but they just flew out of reach. All the rest of the way he kept saying, "I almost had two of 'em!" Camp was cold and windy, and we went to bed hungry as always, but spirits were better. I felt a little left out, because Penny and Katy were laughing and talking in the tent, and Bob and Bill were sitting by the fire, so I just went to sleep.

June 21

I never want another day like this one. Weather was nice but clouds still rolled in and out, never revealing a view. But we were so depleted we could hardly move. I began to get very languid after a mile. Bill just heaved his ice axe out of frustration. He does most of the leading, since he's so good at finding the trail, so he's more depleted than the rest of us. The human body just can't go on like this. I honestly could not stop thinking about food for a second. I got way behind and, as lunchtime passed and I still could not catch up, I had the feeling of being abandoned. It was a nightmare. When I found them, I just dropped my pack without a word and began mixing pudding. I feel so useless.

"... the pudgy bird cruised along on its feet just out of reach."

We had to climb a ridge to find the trail, and from there the hike was fairly steady. I couldn't wait to get to camp and fix dinner. Right when we were about to get to Lake Sally Ann, we saw Robert — a balding blond with muscular legs, loud voice, tiny eyes. Very organized. He is a friend of the three and came out to meet them, since he hiked the PCT north-south last year. Against all wishes, he persuaded us to hike another three miles to Cady Pass. I don't really remember those three. But halfway there, lo and behold he stopped and gave each of us four apple-fig Newtons and a fingerful of peanut butter and honey. I would have followed him anywhere after that. We all just sat there humming and munching. It wasn't much, but it was the best Newton I'd ever had.

Right before Cady Pass I lost the rest of them, as we were dropping out of snow and so had no footprints. Again I got so mad and frustrated I almost lost control, but after twenty minutes of calling I got back with them. That night we decided to try for Stevens Pass early, so I munched out on noodles, freeze-dried, and Robert donated a couple cups of sour cream macaroni. All the while he was talking. He loves to talk. But I went to bed with a full stomach. I felt like I could go anywhere as long as I had food.

June 22

The marathon. I ate almost all my breakfast left in the pack — felt great. We got started at eight and just kept going through snow up to Saddle Gap, and eventually to Pear Lake after an almost straight uphill climb up through Frozen Finger Gap. A lot of lunch next to the lake, and then we began to get lost down in a low area around Wenatchee Pass. My body had to use the bathroom, and when I had caught up everyone was going straight uphill through trees. Bill had found the trail, and we continued to follow his tracks. Grizzly Peak made a pretty hike at six that night. No trees, a rounded peak, and beautiful views. But the light was fading fast. We saw our first unfrozen lake below us — a beautiful sight — and we could hear sounds from a distant highway.

Then we saw Robert again, and he had candy. Bob and I each got a bag of gumdrops and two sticks of taffy. They were gone very quickly. That held us for a while. We still had a ways to go, and I almost ran the whole way. All the slopes down were small, and we just glissaded down. The ridge of Grizzly Peak was long and hairy though, since snow piled up to make a knife-edge to walk on. We had come about fourteen miles that day so far, all through snow, and so we were very weary. The sun was almost gone. But Robert kept saying, "Just a couple miles further and no snow." When we hit no snow, there was also no sun. We stopped in the pitch black dark and decided what to do next. I voted to stop; I thought it ridiculous to push more miles when we couldn't see. But everyone else voted to move on.

I was seething inwardly because I couldn't see the reason for doing that.

I'll certainly never forget those last three hours. Robert kept saying, "Only a few more hundred feet." But at least he kept us going, even if he did lie. It was eerie crossing streams with one flashlight from the other side showing the way, and the light shining through the ponchos and myriad of twigs. All else was pitch black. And the rain wouldn't stop. I was soaked everywhere to the bone. I kept walking off the side of the trail, almost falling down the slope, and each time I became more angry with the situation. At one stream we came to, my feet stepped into air and I hit my stomach on the trail ledge. Then picking myself up I missed every rock and went ankle deep through water in crossing the stream. In rage, I swung my ice ace into the snow several times. I hated this. Everyone was silent, completely ragged out.

I don't know what kept me going those last two miles; I really felt like a cow, one foot in front of the other, the trail nothing but mud from the rain. I looked straight ahead, just feeling the ground with my feet.

We stopped for a rest, a mile to go. All silence, all black, an occasional sniffle. Katy was silently crying. Her knee was giving her trouble. We developed a kind of camaraderie. When I fell across the stream, she rubbed my head, and now I put my arm around her. The last mile took forever, until Bob said, "Is that a road?" It was. 1:00 A.M. and eighteen and a half miles that day.

It's amazing how one's disposition changes when the destination has been reached. A few stars were visible through the clouds — they were beautiful. Robert gave us the rest of his taffy (thank you, thank you, thank you), and we piled into his car.

Even with a forty-pound pack on my head, I still fell asleep.

The car was warm, and I was sitting down. It was like a heavenly dream to see street lights flash by, especially since I was half-asleep. We pulled into a high school at Leavenworth, grabbed our sleeping bags, and hobbled over next to the wall of the school. Asleep, 3:00 A.M.

June 23

I slept terribly, but we awoke to a hot sun. Someone was mowing around us, and a dog was sniffing about me as I woke up. I was sore and groggy, but the sun put everyone in good spirits. We crammed back into the car and took off for downtown Leavenworth. Robert drove us around and then pulled up to the bakery. For the first time, I could imagine it being summertime; it was about 80°. It was so weird; I honestly thought I had been transported in time.

Over to a gas station for two candy bars. To the grocery store for a bag of potato chips and a pint of milk! Three wonderful trips to the bakery for six assorted blueberry, sour cream, and cherry pastries. We parked ourselves in the middle of town in the grass and then went back to the store for a half-gallon of ice cream. Rocky Road. Then we just lay in the park eating ice cream. Clouds came in and cooled things down — but still a nice day. I talked a while with Michael Duvine, who has been train hopping, just seeing the country for four years. He's about twenty. A real pleasant guy. He told me about how nice train yard workers were; they would tell him the best places to ride on the train. He was very interested in the hike, and we looked at some maps for a while. He was hungry, too. Kept grabbing some ice cream.

How can I explain the joy of entering a grocery store? I was dazzled by the myriad of colors and enormous assortment of food. I really realized what a joy it was to be able to have so much food in one place. I imagine a Cambodian or Pakistani would view the place in the same way. A true luxury. When we

" ... we awoke to a hot sun."

passed the magazine rack, I spied a couple of comic books. Those signified for me all of my previous civilized summers. Shorts, sun, bright skies, readily available food, comfort; Lord, did I miss that.

Robert returned with three pounds of cherries. We washed our clothes, slept, browsed the shops, and then had a campfire dinner of very greasy burgers with cheese, onions, ketchup, mustard, and potatoes with sour cream and butter. Robert had to go, so we said goodbye. What a guy; what a lifesaver. I love him.

Bob and I found a concrete slab behind a church in the middle of the town, but still out of sight, to sleep on. We were right next to a window of a bathroom where these two guys were having a party with two girls, but I was more interested in my newly bought cookies and milk.

June 24

We woke up and went back to the same place for breakfast. I finished off my cookies and milk and some fruit. We organized our packs and made some last hits on the bakery and candy store. We split up to hitchhike back to Stevens Pass. Katy and I started walking, and in fifteen minutes Kurt and Diane stopped in a pickup truck and picked us up. (I didn't know them before; they gave us their names later.) They had hiked the PCT the year before, south to north, and invited us over to show us slides of their trip. I almost fell asleep watching the slides, but a bowl full of strawberries and whipped cream woke me up. They live in a cabin, walls of logs, tapestries hanging on the walls, hanging bedspreads for partitions, a wooden oven for making cherry leather. A neat place.

We rode on to Stevens Pass, where I called home and later talked to Glen Katzenburger, the ranger. Kurt and Diane took us to a hot spring, where we had sandwiches under a slight rain, but the hot spring felt great. It was amazing to be standing nude, knee deep in steaming water with six other naked people. But when your body does not have its basic needs fulfilled — rest and food — any kind of sexual stimulation is nonexistent. I couldn't have cared less; it was completely natural. We slept that night in the snow tunnel of Glen's home, and the rain came harder.

June 25

We hiked in a driving rain, which slowly stopped. Then up into the snow again. Goodby, Leavenworth. Lunch was great. I brought some Braunschweiger for the first couple of days. Right after lunch we came upon a steep slope of short switchbacks that was free of trees, about two hundred feet high, with a sheet of hard snow on it. Bill laughed and glissaded right down — no problem. Penny, a little nervous, got halfway across and slipped. She went into the ice axe arrest, which didn't slow her down at all, and then the axe hung on something and slipped out of her hands. She turned sideways and screamed. She collided into two open switchbacks and rolled to a stop on some broken rock. We were dumbfounded — couldn't say anything. What a helpless feeling to only be able to watch something like that and not be able to help at all. But she lifted her head and said, "Would you believe I'm still alive?" She was unhurt.

I started across and began kicking steps down to get her axe, still in the ice. Then I slipped. I just remember holding onto the axe as hard as I could, but still sliding just as fast, with snow spraying across my face. I turned sideways — all was a blur; landed on my pack — more blur; and then came to a stop on the broken rock. I didn't want to move. Scratched and sore but nothing broken. Bill was losing it though. He just kept laughing. I asked Katy later why he did that, and she said he just lost his nerve. Bob made it down safely, but Katy then fell halfway down. It was frightening. Looked like when on the Wide World of Sports the guy says, "And the agony of defeat," when the skier falls off the jump ramp. Katy had sprained her wrist and got a cut under her eye but was otherwise all right. Bob said, "You guys are damn lucky." We camped early that night.

June 26

A cloudy day, some rain and snow. We got lost next to Surprise Lake; Bill had forged ahead, and we lost his tracks. We ended up hiking a couple of hard miles out of our way. We heard him calling, and way up in the pass we could see his tiny figure as the fog thinned for a minute. The climb up was very steep, but the snow was sloshy and not dangerous. The birds were amazingly courageous. They would dive for our packs when we stopped for a munch break. You could even swing your ice axe at them on a limb, and they wouldn't budge. After slogging down through more snow, we arrived at Deception Lakes and camped a few miles farther at Seventeen Mile Camp. My feet are beginning to really give me a hard time.

June 27

The weather was still cloudy...a bit of rain. For part of the day we descended out of snow and then began the long climb up around Cathedral Peak. A very eerie day, the clouds obscuring most of the peak. The topo map showed a very sharp incline around it, and we were somewhat afraid of what it would be like because of yesterday. But the slope was a southern one and open. We got lost a little but could see the trail through the fog going down. That fall yesterday made me very uneasy around snow slopes. I go much slower. Otherwise, it hasn't affected me too much.

We had a late lunch, 5:00 P.M., and I pigged out on a lot of food. We ate next to Deep Lake, which was low and dry but still very cold from no sun. Bill and Bob tried to fish — no luck. Penny collected frogs for a try at some frog legs for dinner, but they were too small, so we let them go. Twenty frogs in one heap suddenly disperse, like the first shot in a pool game.

We crossed a deep, wide river after lunch. Bill made it fine; Bob and I took off our boots and socks and slogged across. Penny tried to get across by way of the logs and fell thigh-deep in water. Katy was last. Halfway across, the log she was on began floating away, but somehow she made it across dry. Guess what? One hundred yards later another river. Katy and I said, "Forget it," and we slogged across, boots and all. Bob took off his boots again, and Penny slogged across too. Bill had found a tiny tree and tightroped across. We came across a beautiful meadow, decided we couldn't pass it up, and had to camp there.

June 28

A gorgeous mountain! In twenty minutes the sky went from all clouds and fog to perfectly clear. The morning was frosty, cold; no snow, but hard frost. As the sun came over the ridge it would melt the frost, and then the meadow would begin to steam. It was neat to watch the place awaken and warm up. A shorts day! We continued down under a warm sun and clicked off seven miles to Waptus Lake. Lunch on a windy rock with a beautiful view of an uplift mountain — flat on one side like an ironing board. Five miles of switchbacks up and then slogging across a lot of snow brought us to our campsite between switchbacks.

June 29

A nice day, but my feet hurt terribly, so I had to switch to tennis shoes. I lost myself for about a half-hour at the river but got back on the trial. We had lunch on a log by a waterfall, then continued on up to snow. I left my pack on the trail while taking a potty break, and on seeing it sitting there realized for the first time what a beautiful sight that red pack was. It's my home, my food, my warmth; I'm developing a respect for it. We crossed snowfields up to Chickamin Ridge and began the traverse. Very treacherous. Snow chutes at 50° angles cascading hundreds of feet down to rocks below. But no surprises. We also saw mountain goats, three of them. They were a creamy white and could climb straight up the rock slopes. Amazing animals. The wind and clouds forced a depressing march into Huckleberry Saddle.

June 30

A beautiful day. The sky was an electric, deep blue. And around the ridge was a stunning view of Mt. Rainier. It was at least three

" We also saw mountain goats, three of them."

times higher than anything near it and gutted with glaciers, which were scored with huge crevasses. We began seeing people again.

At lunch time came one guy bounding around the ridge. We talked, and he offered Bob and me a ride to his home in Issaquah for a shower and food. Trail was blasted off a knife ridge — very interesting. The slope below us was almost straight down, all rock, about one thousand feet. Thank God there was no snow on it. We made Snoqualmie at 7:00 P.M. Everything was closed. Two guys came to pick up the three and take them to civilization, and Jeff Hogan took Bob and myself to Denny Creek campsite for the night.

July 1

I hate this. Here it is July 15 and I'm still catching up. I'll just skim the details. The thoughts are important. We drove to Issaquah with Jeff, whose mom made us lunch. We browsed in his yard, eating cherries from an abandoned cherry tree. A virtual paradise. After a foray into the grocery store, his mom fixed us dinner. Then we just packed our packs and slept in his basement.

It was very interesting being in a real home for the first time this summer. A house has begun to seem like a box now, and it surprised me how much time this family spent inside. And yet I know I used to spend even more time inside. Also, it really struck me seeing how much food was a part of their life. They had three delicious big meals a day, and they left food on their plates, too. I don't think I could ever do that again. This life seemed like such a luxurious one; I want so badly to be back in it. Just to go one day without hurting feet, or being exhausted by day's end, would be so nice.

July 2

A delicious breakfast, and then back to Snoqualmie (after a quick rampage of a McDonald's). Jeff was very nice to us; we really did appreciate his understanding. I now have a very soft place in my heart for helping out hitchhikers and backpackers. We climbed uphill to Lodge Lake, where we made camp for the night. The packs are seventy pounds. I can't believe I have that much food. I had some kind of cheesecake that night for dessert. It was excellent.

July 3

Ascended into snow, very cold weather, and rain. Spirits were low enough to warrant hiking only six miles that day to Mirror Lake, where we just wrote some and went to sleep.

July 4

This is the day we met the infamous logging road. Katy and I were ahead and began hiking on a trail detour. The trail was obliterated by fallen and burned trees. Such an ugly sight. All the hills are bald. The mountains are low now, much like the Appalachians. We found out we had taken seven miles of detour and only covered one trail mile. Lunch was infested with mosquitoes. I just put on my rain jacket, pulled over the hood, and watched the insects try to get through my wool pants and shirt. One feels so helpless around those things, because there are so many of them and they are so hellishly aggravating.

After lunch Bill, Katy, and I got lost on a logging road near Stirrup Lake. The mosquitoes were unbelievable. Stop for a second, and they would literally attack the face and arms. Clouds of them. We figured that Bob and Penny were ahead of us, so we hurried to catch up. The rain would stop, then start, then stop — all day long. And everywhere the hills had been logged bald. After Stampede Pass we realized Bob and Penny were behind us, because we couldn't find footprints. It was 9:00 P.M. and getting dark, so Bill and I made camp on the trail using his ground cloth. Because it was late, we just had gorp for dinner. We walked twenty miles that day. I thought about Mom and Dad at the Peachtree Road Race, and I thought of the farm.

July 5

Bob and Penny came up behind us at nine that morning. Turns out they had gotten lost too and had been behind us all that time. But no one had water. We had to hike about a mile before we found a stream. Our first experience with real thirst. Oregon's going to be tough if it's like this. The rest of the day we just kept hiking the roads and eventually camped that night on a dead-end dirt road. Very windy.

July 6

We decided to forget the detours and try to strike out on our own. We lost our way for awhile but ultimately found the trail after about forty-five minutes. Moving was very slow; all the debris and fallen trees just impeded any progress we could make. Six miles of the trail was road again, but these miles passed quickly. We skirted Pyramid Peak and finally arrived at Government Meadow. Our second consecutive day of beautiful weather.

I forgot about a July 2 entry. I talked to one climber at Snoqualmie Pass who had just tried to cross Chickamin Ridge. He was very scared and absolutely could not believe we had crossed that. I said, "I guess there's an element of stupidity in doing that." He nodded vehemently. Looking back now, I can better realize how lucky we have been in several places. It makes me embarrassed to think that we have crossed dangerous sections of trail but also happy in a way that we've done something that others more experienced have not been able to do.

The night of July 6 marks a red-letter day. We were about to go to sleep, and I noticed Bob standing around, looking at the stars. Finally he came up to me and said he and Katy were quitting the hike. We talked for about twenty minutes. I admired his decision, because it's difficult to stop doing something when others are excited about your continuing on. I feel like he felt he was losing a certain amount of pride in doing so, but it's also tougher to realize that you aren't getting what you want out of a trip and to forget others' opinions.

This makes me ponder why I'm out here still doing this, because Lord knows I'm not having a good time. I'm happy to have done what I have, in a way happy to have accomplished certain things, and I would never trade these past experiences for anything, ever. But I don't know if I can handle constant fatigue and pain and the thought of being on the trail every day for four and a half more months. My left shoulder's going numb again and my swollen right knee also bothers me. Am I ruining my body for life?

In a way I'm relieved that Bob's leaving. We could not get along. Bob is a quick-tempered person, and three-fourths of the time he was cursing something and at times would be mad at me. I was talking to Katy one time on a logging road, and she said, "Tom, I think Bob has it in his mind that you're going to make him mad, and there's nothing you can do about it." I really felt that way. And it's wearing me down, causing anxiety. I think once he leaves it will be easier, although I hate to say that.

July 7

A beautiful day again. The trail wound up to Arch Rock Shelter, where we strolled through beautiful meadows. Clover and flowers provided bright splotches of brilliant color. For the first time I felt like I was in country I had come here to see. And no more logging. We have now learned to appreciate very much the green forests below us. How beautiful they are! We finished the day with a tired tromp into Big Crow Basin. Along the way we did find large, vertical outcrops of black rock which provided for some rock climbing and pictures. I found a rock I think Granny would like. We saw seven elk pass on the ridge above us tonight. Threatening clouds, but they scattered.

July 8

Another clear day. We climbed up to a pass, which gave a breath-taking view of Rainier. There was some ash at the base. And the glaciers; they were gutted and slashed with vicious crevasses. We could look to our right and see the Olympic Mountains. And behind us were the snowcapped peaks we had fought for thirty days. What a view.

We had an early lunch, then a hike to Sheep Lake for a rest, and then on to Chinook Pass. A man and his wife, the Ham Rideouts, gave Bob, Katy, and myself a ride while Bill and Penny hiked on to White Pass. A very nice couple with a very wet dog, which slept in our laps in the back seat. He dropped off Katy and myself — handing us some fresh trout — and brought Bob on to Longmire. A pickup truck full of empty beer cans and three

*"A pickup truck full of empty beer cans and three hairy
huge guys in the cab brought us to Highway 12..."*

hairy, huge guys in the cab brought us to Highway 12, and then
a fat old fisherman in a station wagon carried us on to White
Pass.[10]

We had a great time there. A rock slide knocked out the power
in the Cracker Barrel Grocery, so we got all the ice cream we
wanted. A whole gallon and four Nutty Buddies for two people.
Yum. Katy was kind of mad, because we talked to a guy who's
planning on hiking the PCT next year. He was getting down on
her for quitting. People just can't realize what it's like to hike
like this and don't know how justified someone is in stopping.
We seem to be disillusioning a lot of people who want to hike
it in the future.

July 9

We camped in deep ash from St. Helens and ate the fish given
us by Ham Rideout. Delicious. We had a box of crackers from

the store and then started back down the highway. No rides until finally an old couple picked us up. Very nice; took us to see the Palisades. They were just columns of rock hanging down over a gorge; looked like curtains hanging down. Then another old couple picked us up, then two girls, then a Cajun. At 5:00 P.M. we were in Longmire under terrible weather. Just drizzle and no sights. Couldn't even see Mt. Rainier, which was now fifteen miles away. Katy got a ride on with the Cajun couple, while Bob and I made camp at Cougar Rock campground.

July 10

Our climb up Rainier began today. We had a slow, pleasant hike up to Narada Falls, where a man and his three blond sons gave us a ride to Paradise Visitor Center. Still all fog. We walked around, looking at exhibits, and had a bite in the cafeteria. I badly want to climb the mountain, but it's $125 for a guide per person. We registered with a ranger to let him know we were going to go at least up to Camp Muir. Ranger Steve Ross gave us some pointers, taught us how to do the boot-axe belay and use prusiks,[11] and then we started up. I hate Bob's attitude. At first he's gung ho about climbing it. Then when he finds out the price, he says, "No way in hell I'm going." Then he decides he might. Then he refuses. Now he wants to again. I wouldn't mind if he didn't make such a big deal about changing his mind. We walked a trail, partially in snow, up to 7,200 feet, where we made camp at Pebble Creek. The strong wind blew the tent down, so we just pulled out the poles. Then came the rain. We didn't get a wink of sleep that night, especially with the wind rattling the tent like that. Once, at one in the morning, the fog split for a second to reveal a huge black cloud cap obscuring the summit and black clouds below us. At eye level was a blaze of stars. But it lasted only a second.

July 11

We started again, through snow the rest of the way to Camp

Muir. The weather was miserable — cold wet rain, dense fog, and high winds. Man, was I depressed. I just wish I knew for sure if we would be able to climb or not. We got lost for a half hour until finally Camp Muir emerged at ten thousand feet. We stashed our equipment in the rock shelter there as seventeen other climbers came up. Turns out they did have room for two more. I wasn't sure if I did want to climb, after that terrible weather.

Muir marked the place where the snow fields end and the crevasses begin. I looked out on the Cowlitz Glacier and could see several long crevasses cut into it. I just ate dinner and fell asleep while it began to snow outside. One guy had carried a hibachi up, and his group was cooking steaks. Yum. When darkness fell, three climbers came down who had been at the summit. They looked dead tired. I remember seeing one of them sitting with the light of his stove silhouetting him, quietly drinking hot chocolate. Earlier that day we had met two groups that had abandoned the climb.

July 12

We woke at 3:30 A.M. I munched on some breakfast and got my pack together. At that elevation, even putting on crampons required a few pauses in between each movement to catch your breath. But the sky — dark purple — was ablaze with stars. There was a sea of clouds about two thousand feet below us, and we could see Mt. St. Helens with a large plume of smoke silhouetted in the lights of Portland. It was snapping cold, too, about 30°.

Mr. Rand, the party leader, led us in prayer, and we then began at 5:00 A.M. The guide service had gone on before us; we could see a tiny string of lights as they went across the Cowlitz Glacier with their flashlights.

The snow was frozen this early, and we climbed up the Cathedral Rocks after crossing the glacier. At the top of the rocks we paused on Ingraham Glacier for a rest. The sun was rising, creating a spectrum of colors along the horizon. Behind us we could see Mt. Adams, Mt. Hood, and St. Helens; and in front we could see Glacier Peak. Above the glacier was a jumble of huge seracs — about the size of ten-story buildings.

We climbed up the steep Disappointment Cleaver among a forest of sharp, tall suncups,[12] shedding clothing as the sun came up. At the top of the Cleaver, five of the seventeen had to turn back because of altitude sickness. I was switched to another rope, and we continued up. Bob and I felt better than the rest, I guess because of our conditioning.

The crevasses were awesome. At times we would pass a little hole, peer in, and find out we were walking over a huge ice cave. Some crevasses were hundreds of feet deep. Down in them the ice became a blue-green. Long icicles along the edge gave them the appearance of lipless jaws — horrible smiling slits in the ice. We crossed a snow bridge and jumped three crevasses. Each time we belayed each other with the ice axe. This required a four-foot jump, and for a split second in midair you could look straight down the crevasse.

It was getting cold; the wind was picking up and ice crystals flashed around our faces. The sky was a very dark blue now, and clouds way below us obscured the ground. On up. Eventually we could see the summit, and before I knew it, we were at the rim of a huge crater about three hundred yards wide. It was filled with snow, but the craggy rocks around the rim had windblown ice sticking horizontally off the sides. Winds also fashioned the ice into little scallop shapes. I left my pack on the crater rim, walked across the crater, and was the third person to reach the 14,410-foot summit dome (10:50 A.M.). Clouds all around, way below us, and a cold, cold wind. But what an exhilaration to be at the top. Bob and I took pictures as the rest slowly came up. Everyone fell into his own quiet, tired reverie. It was neat to see the first one up wait for another and then grasp hands as they stepped on the summit. This type of experience forms camaraderie like that. It's one of the greatest things that has happened to me.

After a half-hour we had to descend. The rope leader made me furious. He insisted on running down the mountain, and being on the end of the rope, I was getting whipped around every corner and going into slides down the mountain. I don't even know when I've been so full of anger, being dragged down the mountain without choice. It took us two hours to get back to Muir, and there we rested for a couple of hours before descending back to Paradise.

Bob and I had a good talk on the way down, and he said something that explains a lot about him. He said he has one view of true human nature, and that's that all people are greedy. I imagine he found me very greedy because he was looking for it and so would get mad for that reason. I personally feel sorry for him if he thinks that way about all people.

We tried to relax at the Paradise Hotel; but the influx of people got to us, and we left. I was again depressed, just because I wanted to be home. I was tired of people looking at me like I'm from outer space, knowing they were on their way back to their own homes in a few hours. After talking awhile with a couple until dark, we threw out our bags by the roadside and went to sleep.

July 13

This morning I gazed up at Mt. Rainier under a clear sky. I couldn't believe I had been to the top of that thing. We hitched a ride down to Longmire again with an older couple who were very interested in our trip. After lunch and getting the food boxes, we got a ride all the way to Yakima to begin our detour of Mt. St. Helens. We had heard that the ash messed up equipment, was up to three feet deep, and that one week of breathing it was equivalent to twenty years of smoking. Besides that, there was a ranger turning people away, so we decided to detour. A couple named Barbara and I-forget-his-name gave us a ride, and we ate at some cafe along the way; and then they left us in an apple orchard (fruit not ripe yet) next to the highway. I hate hitchhiking; I just like to know how I'm going to get somewhere and when. This night was one of my most anxious. I didn't think we'd be able to make the trip and yet without that goal I felt like an irresponsible waste just roaming the west. Lord, was I down. I really wonder what Mom and Dad think of me: that I've degenerated and am spending their money or what. I did a good bit of agonizing that night.

July 14

I called Mrs. Hull[13] from a Texaco station near our campsite. We met her, her husband, and their son Phil. They took us to eat at a place called VIPs and then all the way to Cascade Locks, Oregon, the end of our detour[14] around St. Helens. Talking to them was such a boost for morale because of their interest in the trip. I guess they're the first Christians I've met on the trip. What a refreshing time, and how neat to cruise over dry flatlands. This really looks like the West.

We arrived at Cascade Locks and found Bill. He told us two Indians had stolen Penny's pack last night, so that would delay us a couple more days. But what a pain to her. She's getting money from her mom, though; but still, very aggravating. I put my pack in the tent tonight. It's refreshing also to be back with Penny and Bill.

Cascade Locks to Callahan's

> What a day this is! How many impressions have flashed through my mind, from the moment I started the nails from the painted boards of the "home box," until now that I hear a wild wind blowing and can see myriads of dead leaves darting and tumbling through the air like live things!
>
> N. C. Wyeth, **The Wyeths**

July 15

A great, lazy day. I wrote, ate, slept, ate, called home, ate, etc. Bob and I went to Stevenson to get my food drop. Hallelujah! Cheese Straws![15] I love you, Mamma! And extra M&Ms and cheese, too. I felt bad after calling Mom and Dad, because Dad said, "Now you promised us you wouldn't climb Rainier without a guide," and after they heard about Bob stopping, Mom implored me not to hike by myself. I felt bad, but the call did me good, just to talk to them.

I think Rainier took a bigger toll on me that I thought. I'm getting sick, my knee's pretty sore, and my lips are cracking a lot. But it's nice to relax here. This place is pretty. I ate a whole frozen Boston cream pie by myself. Yum.

July 16

Slept late. Ate doughnuts, wrote, and read all day while Penny and Katy hitched to Portland to get her a new pack. Bob found a six-hour job pulling weeds at the grocery store. For some reason, I've been sleeping a lot; I guess it's just the cold. A good, relaxing day.

July 17

Slept lots again. The itch to make miles is coming back; and, even though we like being here, we're eager to move. The packs are heavy — too heavy, even allowing for food. It worries me because I only hiked two and a half miles, and it felt like twelve. I can't wait until they get lighter.

We camped at Eagle Creek. When I was brushing my teeth, an old man came up and said, "I'm doing the same thing as you except a little different," and he pulled out his dentures.

I had bought a book at Cascade Locks, one I've always wanted to read, called *Dune*.[16] The mind needs to be able to play, so it's nice to have.

July 18

Finally an early start, at eight. The trail for the first seven miles could not have been prettier. We passed Punch Bowl Falls, where the water poured through a round depression in the rock, then over an overhang. The rock almost looked as if it had been sculpted. At times the slope dropped vertically to a precipitous one hundred feet. All rock faces were covered in moss. At Tunnel Falls the trail went into a cave behind a 150-foot waterfall and then out on the other side. We continued up the gorge until the creek was deep and wide but still very beautiful with a wealth of possible swimming holes. At one point we stood at the top of a fall overlooking the valley. A very beautiful hike. It's amazing how often I thought of the farm — and how many experiences there I recall. One certain sight, sound, or smell, and whole moments at the farm will flash back, and I almost feel like I'm there ....

The last six miles were hell. Straight up, three thousand feet with flies and mosquitoes flying up nostrils and in eyes. It's amazing how such a beautiful day can turn into such a hellish one. We camped at Indian Springs.

July 19

The trail began in an area that had burned in the 1920s and so was bald — but green. A huge cloud cover right at head level obscured all but the base of Mt. Adams, about fifty miles north. A pretty morning. Now, as we're in lower altitudes, it's definitely summertime. We hear katydids and feel hot sun, sweating the uphills. It's amazing — I guess it's because the farm was my first exposure to wilderness, but I had many quiet reveries thinking about that place.

Our first view of Hood. It's an awesome mountain; looks like something out of Tolkien. It slopes slightly and then shoots sharply to a peak. The only snow-covered mountain around. Our trail gave us closer and closer views of it; tomorrow the trail goes around the base.

My feet hurt like crazy again. I guess it's just the pack weight. And now mosquitoes join the scenery. They attack now even when I'm hiking. I put on my mosquito net hat before I went insane. We camped just past Lolo Pass.

July 20

The mornings are beautiful. I got a head start and had such a good time hiking alone. It's so different when one is alone — each little rift and valley has its own mystery and personality. But it sure was getting hot. Katy caught up eventually, and we

Cascade Locks to Callahan's/59

"Our first view of Hood."

had a good time talking as we traversed a ridge to big glacial streams. We had excellent views of Mt. Hood, as we were now at its base. The white icy summit looked like a cutout against that blue sky. Crossing the rivers was a trembling experience because there were no bridges, but boulder hopping was fun and added spice to the day. We had lunch just past Ramona Falls. We saw the falls and about thirty people. There is a trail two miles long from a road, and so many people can get there. The falls were pretty, though, about one hundred feet high and built up by moss-covered rocks, like building blocks, over which the water ran.

Bill and I were the studly hikers and were going to make it all the way to Timberline Lodge that night. But, presto: we took a wrong trail and hiked three miles out of our way. The trail had no water, and the heat was about 100°, so the detour wiped me out. Bill kept on, though. I camped with the others at a nice spot about three miles from the falls. I wish I could keep circumstances from ruling my disposition, because that detour — and usually most mishaps — really color my view of the trip. I was a raging maniac after getting lost. I seem to be losing control of my temper. I need to work on that. What a hot day.

July 21

Up, up, up. The trail doesn't stop going up. Katy and I were ahead again, but still this uphill stifled all conversation. No relief. We came to Slide Mountain and Sandy River Canyon. It looked like the desert. A high wind in the canyon whipped dust all around us. We could hardly see anything; all was obscured by dust. And the yellow sun popping over Mt. Hood promised another blazing day. But the trail continued up to alpine meadows ... beautiful. After being in the forest for awhile, these brilliant green meadows were very refreshing. Blazing blue sky and green hills. From the crest of a ridge we saw Mt. Jefferson on the horizon, with his flanks covered with snow. Mt. St. Helens stood distantly behind us — a blackish brown flattened mountain. Looked almost like a mesa.

We almost got lost again but got straightened out and descended into Zigzag Canyon. Lord, what idiot devised this trail? Just up-down, up-down. It's so discouraging to hike downhill and lose all the elevation that twenty minutes before you had sweated so hard to gain. I kept going and had lunch alone, but they caught up soon and we hiked on uphill to Timberline Lodge. We easily got rides down to Government Camp, only to find that

Penny and I had left our ice axes back at Timberline. I went back, but they were gone. The monetary aspect doesn't bother me, but that axe and I had been through so much together — I feel like I've lost a friend.

We played Monopoly after dinner (a trail dinner) in a ski lodge that a friend of Bill's opened up for us here in Government Camp. What fun and luxury! Because of the dry trail and heat we get filthy easily, and so a shower was unadulterated joy. As I rested in the lodge I heard "Sailing" playing on the stereo. That was my favorite song before I had left. I guess it's a hit now.

Recently I've developed a need to be alone. I look forward to being with just Bill and Penny, and even at lunch I forged ahead so I could eat alone. Oregon should be easy, and I want to make miles. But it bothers me, because I told Mom and Dad I wouldn't hike alone. Bill said he needs to fix his pack, get it sent to the factory — will take ten days. I want to hike ahead alone and let them catch up, but how can I do that when parents that I've come to appreciate and love so much don't want me to? It can be so lonely — I can't tell anyone for fear it'll get to them. The other four can't understand.

July 22

We had saunas and Monopoly last night — lots of fun. All I did was read *Dune*, write letters, and sleep. I also bought a dozen eggs and a loaf of bread. It was great.

July 23

Still here at the lodge. We're getting antsy, eager to move, and Bill has decided not to send his pack; but their food drop hasn't arrived yet. I went up to Timberline to try to get some equipment to climb Mt. Hood, but not in time. We played Risk tonight. It was fun, but we got pretty sleepy.

July 24

Still no food drop. Bob, Bill, and I rented some equipment and began up Palmer Glacier on Hood to the top of the ski lifts. We had a good time up there, with the wind blowing hard, just eating some gorp and laughing and talking. We tried to sleep at 5:00 P.M. but found it hard. Bill would start laughing on his own, without anyone saying a word, every once in a while. We kept waking periodically as clouds rolled in below us.

July 25

We awoke to bright moon, almost full, at two. It was cold. It took a while to tie in, but we got started at three, right when the moon sank. With little light we stumbled up to Hogsback Ridge. A silver dawn appeared, showing white clouds below and catching the top of Mt. Jefferson, some fifty miles away. We passed Crater Rock, which cradled a hole with yellow-green rock that emitted fumes of sulfur — the steam rising high and smelling of eggs.

Crossing the Bergschrund required a long, wide step, and after that we climbed an almost vertical wall of ice up to the summit. I had cramps right before the top and had to kneel down and lean to one side, but that helped. The view was a little disappointing: a thick haze obscured almost everything, but I was glad I had come. Early morning is so beautiful; I love watching the day unfold. After a bite we descended, and on down we watched skiers schuss back and forth. A few on the ski lift above were curious about the climb and asked us about it.

Back at the lodge we had a sauna (ah, joy) and shower. (On the ride down to the lodge a guy in a dump truck picked us up. We just stood on a little ledge about a foot wide as he bounced and jounced on down the road. Then he picked up two more hitchhikers, and we laughed and yelled and hung on for dear life the rest of the way.)

I registered for the draft today.

Penny's feet hurt badly; she doesn't want to continue and is kind of bummed out about the trail. She says Bill may quit soon too. And I've been thinking about how I can hike sixteen hundred miles without Mom and Dad knowing I'm alone. I get so frustrated — it seems like everything is trying to end this trip.

I also am going to have to leave behind the superhook and cheese cloth — just no room. This also got me, because I think about Mom buying it for me, thinking of all these things it could do for me — and I have to leave it. I want this thing over with.

July 26

Food is here! At last! I packed up and took some garbage down and cleaned up some. Bob and I shook hands; "It's been real," he said. "Yeah, that's the word for it." He nodded. "That's the best word for it." He wished us luck, and we promised to meet later on down the trail, although I know we won't. I hugged Katy and took off. A black Capri gave me a ride to Barlow Pass, where I started out. Bill and Penny were coming later, and we're going to meet tonight. It was so neat to be alone for those thirteen miles. I'm able to make better time and feel freer and more confident. It's good to be back on the trail, making distance towards my goal. The trail is dry and stays in a low forest, where at times mosquitoes abound. I found a deep, cold spring, where a frog dropped in as I dipped my water cup in. But soon I was at Little Crater Lake, where I waited for Bill and Penny. Just off the trail was a pond, perfectly clear and very cold. Beautiful. Unfortunately, it was near a road, and there were about twenty people watching some guy trying to scuba dive, but they left after awhile.

A full moon tonight. It's beautiful — a silver-splotched orb, right above the tree tops. I can't believe man has been there. It's quieter now without Bob and Katy; it definitely seems like something is missing. Ice axe gone too. This is truly a new time now. I slept alone in the tent; it's nice to have so much room.

July 27

I got started before they did and really enjoyed striking off alone. I can make so much better time this way. The mosquitoes are getting bad. Just watching them compete to dive their proboscises into your skin is maddening. So I whizzed quickly by Clackamas River and on a few more miles.

I knew it would happen sooner or later, but I didn't expect this soon. In two hours Penny and Bill caught up, and Bill said, "We've decided to stop; we're leaving at Santiam Pass." I don't know why, but I was even a little excited. They just ate their lunch and everything remained normal. There're so many things going through my head now, so many options. If I want to hike alone; if so, how to tell my parents. I just can't come to a decision.

The waterless trail got to us, and we had a sweaty heavy-breathing slog down to Warm Springs River. We camped next to a nice spring there. We could hear a grunting and yelping and tree shaking in the woods across a meadow. Bill was very curious as to what it was, a little scared. Penny and I crept up to cross the meadow, and it seemed as if the whole forest shook as a massive herd of elk began to take off. The whole herd ran by our tents later that night.

> *There was a little clipclop of sound and dead silence once more, but this time I heard a low uneasy snuffling that could only come from many noses. I groped in the dark for a stick or a stone but could find none. I ran three steps back in a threatening manner and raised a dreadful screech that caused some shifting of feet and a little rumble of menacing sound. The screech had nearly shattered my own nerves. My heart thumped as I tried to recover my poise.*
>
> *Cattle.*
>
> Loren Eiseley,
> **The Night Country**

I got up, got my things together. We swapped addresses and worked out some last minute things, and I got ready to leave. They didn't want to continue the pace since they were stopping, so I had to strike off alone.

Penny stood up as I was about to leave. We hugged each other, and I said, "How do you say goodbye to someone you fell down a mountain with?" My eyes were burning a little. Then Bill stood there with his goony grin, tongue cocked to one side, and I noticed his eyes were a little red too. He's such a great guy. When relaxed, he looks so goony and funny, but he's a tough mountain person at heart. I can't believe he's quitting now. Maybe they're going to get married. We shook hands, and I left.

The trail made a waterless climb up to North Pinhead Butte, and there was Mt. Jefferson on the horizon. With bad spirits caused by a stomach ache and hurting feet, I tromped on to Trooper Springs and had lunch. The six-miler to Jude Lake was easy and pleasant — how quickly one's mood changes in a few hours! The last three miles around Olallie Butte came slowly, and again I was cursing the trail up to the dirt road S12. There was a nice camp on the other side of the road. My first pangs of loneliness. Suppertime and no one around. But bingo — I ventured down the dirt road; and there was Olallie Lake, full of weekend boaters, and a small store, where I got a candy bar and a can of orange juice. That helped a lot.

July 28

I felt good and hiked fast. Man, passing Upper Lake I was attacked by a swarm of mosquitoes, the worst one yet. There was a gorgeous meadow with Mt. Jefferson standing there in all its glory, and I was sprinting by and up a hill as the skeeters kept coming. I got to rest at Many Lakes Viewpoint as the swarm thinned out.

The terrain is becoming very unusual as I enter volcano country. I'll see a butte shoot straight up from the ground, perfectly symmetrical, or a mountain slope of bright red pumice. Very striking. The climb up to Jefferson Park finally put me back in high alpine country, all the way up a snow bank to almost seven thousand feet. And Jefferson Park below — a huge green meadow dotted with trees and lakes and flanked on either side by snow covered slopes — beautiful. And lots of people. I camped about a mile from the park. I like being alone. It's nice to regulate myself, and it's also easier to hike this way.

July 29

I hope I never have to do this again, but I hiked about twenty-four miles today. It was beautiful and varied, but it whizzes past in my mind now because I hiked by so fast. And it's impossible to enjoy a sight when you hurt so bad and feel sick. I had lunch looking over beautiful Hunts Cove after talking to a couple of guys for awhile about the hike. Then up at North Cinder Peak to my left was a wild valley of twisted and contorted lava flows and mounds, with a perfectly flat, huge table off to one side which was capped with a meadow. I could see South Cinder Peak, Three Fingered Jack, Mt. Washington, and the Three Sisters — my next week's hike, all at once. All of these were cast in the orange glow of sunset.

I'm scared I too might quit. How can I stand hurting like this for three and a half more months? So many things weigh on me: money, my future, and what this hike is doing in it. After last term, I really am scared to go back to school. It was a nightmare, studying vehemently and getting nowhere; and now thinking of Mom worrying about me, especially when she finds out I'm alone. I just can't hike knowing how troubled she gets. She loves her children so much, and I've come to love and appreciate Mom and Dad so much. An even though I see people in this popular area, I'm still alone. But facing the fact that I stopped before reaching my goal may be too much also. This trip has become too goal oriented. Mexico should not be the end, but a means to the end. But still, even then, I'd know I let one more set of plans fall through. I've never in my life undertaken a project and brought it into completion, and just this once I want to. But am I wasting three months of my life, when I probably should be working and going to school? God help me, I don't know what to do.

> *At the end only two things really matter*
> *to a man, regardless of who he is; and*
> *they are the affection and understanding*
> *of his family.*
>
> Richard E. Byrd, **Alone**

Almost to Minto Pass, two hikers told me about Peter Wirth, who is alone and southbound. Maybe if I could catch up to him.

The mosquitoes attacked again when I discovered my planned campsite was crowded with twenty-three Boy Scouts. No relief at all, something always. If it isn't snow, then it's the relentless whine of mosquitoes around your head and their stinging of your arms. I found a stagnant pond for water and finally dove into my tent at nine.

A curious doe that stood twenty feet from me when I camped kept returning that night, creeping around the site.

July 30

A little thunder and a little spattering of rain woke me. It was so nice to see clouds. Except for Rainier, it's been twenty days since I've seen more than an occasional cloud.

The mosquitoes were horrible. The first two miles were up, and again my spirits sank as I ran up with a cloud around me. At the top of the ridge was Three Fingered Jack — tan-brown rock towering seven thousand feet to a serrated edge, with snow melt rivers below it. This mountain is special to me, a kind of landmark, because I always remembered it in pictures before the trip, and now I was here. After skirting it and grabbing a very fast mosquito-infested lunch, I kept on down to Santiam Pass. I wanted to climb the Jack but decided to keep going on. That's one thing that gets me: I'll probably never be here again, and time doesn't allow one to know some places as intimately as one wishes.

A couple of older women passed by. Robert Dutton back in Leavenworth told us about the Lodge here at Santiam Pass, and I'd been waiting for this for a month. Then I met three hikers who told me the lodge wasn't serving the one night I was going to arrive. I couldn't believe it. I kept meeting hikers coming and going. Most people I would tell I had hiked from Government Camp, but others I told from Canada. It sometimes gets tiring to explain the trip every time you meet someone.

A couple and their two sons gave me a ride down to the lodge, just a mile from the trail. The couple who runs this place, Mr. and Mrs. Patterson, are delightful. Mr. P. said his wife could whip up something to eat. $1.00 for dinner and breakfast, and $2.00 for bed, shower, and laundry. Can't beat that. No one's here — all the campers are on a hike, and so it's just myself and two bikers. Mrs. P. made salad, fruit salad, cole slaw, lima beans, hamburger, ice cream, doughnuts, and bread and jam. It was great. I was stuffed.

These two bikers are neat. One is quiet, thin, and from Atlanta — went to Northside High. Surprise. We talked about how much we missed the Appalachians. The other was stocky, bearded, loud — one who laughed heartily at his own jokes, but a very nice guy. He gave me some instant butter that's just come out. Makes me recall the lady at Ramona Falls who gave me half a sandwich. People who understand.

From a Lewis & Clark 1804 expedition journal posted on the wall here: "Muskeetors verry troublesom..."

"A buck with six-point antlers ran by."

August 1

A new month. Mr. and Mrs. P. gave a bright good morning as I sit on the steps and write. Just remembered: last night two girl campers came back to the lodge; one had the whole Christopher Cross album on tape. Listening to that made the months before the trip come flooding back. I can't wait to get back, but right now I do want to finish — if Mom and Dad will let me.

But today was reckoning day. I hiked through a burned out forest with Mt. Washington beckoning me onward. A buck with six-point antlers ran by. I then met a group of hikers who gave me a whole bowl of cherries. (Yum.) The trail was easy around Mt. Washington, and on the way I met John Marrow, an Englishman who was going north, making about 30 miles a day. I couldn't believe it.

Once out of the forest, I met a wall of black dried lava. The rock was so twisted and contorted into weird shapes and patterns. All one could see were dead trees, which had been obliterated by the lava flow, sticking up out of the black rock. For some reason I had the worst time climbing that thing (Belknap Crater). I just couldn't make myself move; I almost fell asleep. Then, for the first time, it hit me: I'm bored. That's it. I'm just bored. I'm tired of hiking. That time was the first time I felt like I could really go home and not have qualms about it. I can't spend four hundred more dollars to hike the rest of the way when I really don't want to. The rest of the day I was very depressed. To stay on the trail means three and a half more months of this. I just don't know if I could take it.

To leave, however, means admitting defeat. I know no one expects anything of me, but for some reason it still bothers me. I have a kind of nightmare thought of sitting home, talking to Paul.[17] (I don't know why Paul), and his looking at me and saying, "Yeah, Tom, I'm sure it was tough. So that's why you quit." And on my grad school resume — "Left school to hike around in the Cascades; went home, worked for four months." Great. I just don't know if I could take the mental anguish of going home.

The phone call at Crater Lake will determine. That's all.

August 2

I got started at seven-thirty, hiking up and up towards the Three Sisters and around the Yapoah Crater. So neat to see a perfectly smooth, round hill, all tan, and a day moon suspended above it.

Twice I met a man who is hiking to California. Talking to this pleasant person makes hiking so much easier.

But Lord, doesn't it ever, ever, ever QUIT? My right heel hurts like hell. I couldn't stand it and had to stop after only twelve miles. How can I ever get anywhere with delay after delay after delay?

August 3

Still hurts, but at least made sixteen miles today. During lunch I talked to a big, fat hiker who was going through Oregon. He was amiable but dirty; kept talking about meeting prostitutes on the trail in the Sierra. Weird trail afterwards though. I wound past the Rock Mesa, a frozen tidal wave of lava, and through the Wickiup Plain. I could see the trail for a mile ahead over this plain. It wavered in the distance as heat rose from the ground, but a good view atop Koosah Mountain made me stop for the night.

The mind works in unusual ways when one is alone. My thoughts have been in a constant volley as to whether I even want to continue or not, despite what Mom and Dad say. At times I want to continue, but usually I don't. It's horrible. My dreams have become nightmares; once I dreamed I was back at Davidson, taking remedial courses; another time I was back home, and everyone had their backs turned towards me. These dreams wear on the mind during the day, and they seem to be reality. I begin to miss things so intensely; I feel like I'm missing out on so much, like my life has ended. And the choices — every one of them seems to be terrible. To stay here, to hike alone for three more months, to continue to lose weight and become introverted — is that why I'm out here? To go home and find all I've missed so much, but to realize that I didn't do it. This dream of mine for years, I didn't do it. It seems like everything collapses in any direction.

August 4

I decided not to put up with mosquitoes. The worst is yet to come, so I dropped down to the highway. Eleven miles of highway was not what I needed. The paved road hurts the feet, so it took me most of the day just to do that. I read *Dune* as I walked, kind of weaved along the road, stepping aside for cars. It can be nice to see people, but the knowledge that they are on their way to see familiar faces and stay at a familiar place — that they're on vacation — makes it difficult when I see them. I camped next to a logging road. Sometimes I know I'm just feeling sorry for myself, but I wonder — what exactly would Mom and Dad think if they knew a Marshburn was sitting at a crossroads hungry and exhausted and lonely as hell?

August 5

I got a late start, continuing up the logging roads, and asked some campers about a fork in the road. They were such pleasant company that I stayed for an hour and a half. They gave me coffee, apples, granola bars, and I enjoyed talking with them. Encounters like that make the loneliness increase, but still they're refreshing. I finally got the logging roads behind me and arrived back at the trail. Irish Lake was beautiful — the water was extremely blue. I later visited for about five minutes with a hiker who told me of all the glories of the Sierra in California.

The trail is quite deserted now and is still quite boring. I came to a realization of some of my problems tonight. I stood on a rockpile above my campsite, and there was snow-robed Diamond Peak above a deep, green forest. Blue, blue sky. I thought, now how many people have wanted to see something like this? But I realized, even though the sight was beautiful, it just wasn't home. Nothing out here is familiar. There is nothing one can latch onto and be guaranteed he will see tomorrow; nothing to become a base. That's one problem. I need the rolling hills and hardwood trees of the east — Lord, I miss home and being back there. My favorite place is inside my tent. It's the only environment I can control and call home.

August 6

I got a late start but was able to really cook. My feet feel better, so I made about three miles an hour through swampy mosquito land to lunch at the Rosary Lakes. My thoughts are constantly, every second of my waking hours, in a volley. I want to go home, I should go home; I want to stay, I should go home, I should stay here — on and on. I arrived at Cascade Summit just before five, just in time to grab my package. It was a lot of fun to look at it and explore it, as always; but again, it made me terrifically homesick. I realized that I just don't like this terrain — these low, rolling hills. They're like a mockery of the east, because even though they look somewhat like the Appalachians in shape, there are no hardwoods — only the straight, conical evergreens everywhere.

I called the Bells.[18] Although I wanted to speak to Mr. and Mrs. Bell as well, Gaye was the only one I spoke to. I told her about being alone, being lonely — in a way I got some things off my chest. It helped. It was weird hearing her talk about Atlanta. I realized the summer was almost over, and how short that was for them; it's seemed like a year to me. So Neale is still dating that girl. I miss him and everyone. I think of my clean, fresh friends in nice clothes going to church and dancing and eating — God, I miss that. I'm kind of afraid I'll lose my missing it forever, that I'll go back and not care about these things any longer. These things are special now; I want them to always be that way. After a quart of milk, an ice cream bar, and a burrito, I made camp.

August 7

A very late start, about twelve. I sewed a ripped place in my belt, wrote letters, and finally got started. The land is getting more and more desolate: sparse trees and sandy ground. That's all. Had lunch at Diamond View Lake (the mosquitoes are really bad), and then slogged on until at five I arrived at Crescent Lake. Another resort. I broke down and cried. Never have I missed home and felt so out of place in my life. I camped at Forest Service campground and met a big, fat man who was hiking Oregon. Nice guy, a bird watcher. I had to hand it to him, to be that big and really enjoy hiking. He came over and we talked awhile until dark. Going to bed is great; it's the only time your mind can rest — an eight hour break with no worries.

August 8

The man gave me three freeze-dried dinners — a real treasure. I got started at seven-thirty and hiked on up, higher and higher, but still very much in a desert. My watch stopped. It now has 10:05.05 forever printed on its face. A real loss; I didn't know I had depended on it so much.

I got some water at Nip and Tuck Lakes and scared two ducks. That was a memorable moment for some odd reason — watching one duck flutter by high up, cross in front of the sun, his breath whirring.[19] No views today, just a good climb up to lusher forests. I met two guys on horseback, the first to do the whole PCT in one season on horseback. They said they were going to write a book, and they told me all about California as well.

It was a little difficult to see them riding, carrying nothing at all, but I realized it was pretty brave to bring something as valuable as horses on this trail, like taking care of two people. One guy had been bitten on the boot by a Mojave rattler — most poisonous in America.[20] Lucky to survive.

My camp was excellent. I found a shelter at Maidu Lake and put up a candle. It's amazing what that one little flame can do for your spirits — so soft, slowly undulating, warm, and bright. It was like a little person assuring me that everything was all right. I hated to blow it out, to see the night clamp shut around me. But such complete silence. The Big Dipper was framed perfectly outside the shelter where I could see it from where I lay.

August 9

Up and hiking. I followed the long trail up Tipsoo Peak, again, volleying my desire to go home or not. I can't wait for the call home from Crater Lake. It'll mean so much. Once I sat real still during a break and closed my eyes, imagining myself at the farm. The sounds, but not the sights, closely approximate those at the farm.

Seven thousand six hundred and fifty — the highest point in elevation of the Oregon-Washington PCT was attained today. Up again into meadows, but I hardly noticed the altitude. Water is very sparse; the knowledge that you have so little adds to your thirst. It was very pleasing to finally come across Thielsen Creek. Lots of cool water. Late lunch there with Mt. Thielsen towering three thousand feet above me, "The Lightning Rod of the Cascades." I was looking forward to climbing it; it was supposed to be easy. I went up the wrong way, though, and fought very loose rock and sand, cursing and sweating, and then gave up. Every step almost caused an avalanche. I later found out I had gone the wrong way — what a waste. On the way down the trail I could see the rim of Crater Lake — amazing. Looked exactly like the top of a mountain had been blown off, leaving the edges and a deep bowl, although I couldn't see the lake itself.

August 10

A morning surprise. While I'm using the bathroom behind a tree (oh, no one will walk by), a girl comes hiking up. Marlis is going Mexico-Canada, the second person I've met on foot so far. We talked for a good while. Apparently I'm the only one left who has made it all the way from Canada.

The hike today was long and low and very, very dry. I went almost fifteen miles on two cups of water. It gave me a bad headache and really wore me out. My mind was filled with thoughts of my favorite drinks. The capability of drinking — the flowing muscle action of the throat — seems like such a heavenly gift. Red Cone Spring was cool and very welcome; I was at my wits end when I got there. After a good dinner there was much light left, so I went cross-county up to the rim. The first mile was forest, which drove me crazy as I followed deer trails and stepped over old rotten tree trunks. The way opened before me, and I stood at the edge of a vast inclining plain. Although three miles away it looked like the top of the hill, I knew I was looking at the crater rim. Snow even — a little on the edge. I couldn't wait to get there. But the walk was long. A flat plain like that distorts perspective, and it took me one and a half hours to get across. Damnable little molehills kept giving way under me, and I set my eyes on a lone tree and headed for it. I was also heading towards a distant antlered deer. It spotted me when I was a hundred yards away and trotted off. It was so quiet there. I turned around at the tree and could see down the plain, back to the trees a mile away, an immense red shaft of billowy clouds reflecting the last of the sun. The rest of the sky was blackening. Mt. Thielson was on the horizon, very dreamlike in the half-light. I stood there and said, "I think I could get to like Oregon." With that testimonial to a beautiful sunset, I continued on up the plain. When I reached the rim drive it was night. I now stepped on up to the rim. My Lord. A roar of space hit me as I looked at a mile-wide lake two thousand feet below. The wind in the crater swept me, and it was fantastic. After a minute, though, my mind quickly changed to a place far away — Mom and Dad drinking their coffee and watching T.V. Sadly I laid out my bag in a grove of dilapidated trees, with a view fit for gods at my feet. Tonight was a meteor shower, and I caught a few out of the corner of my eye before I fell asleep. Tonight was also the battle with the chipmunks. They just kept coming. In my half sleep, they'd rip bags and snicker and chirp and piddle around; and I'd whack my pack with a stick, cursing and yelling, and they'd dive away; and five minutes later it'd happen again. I wish I had a .22. I hate those things. A car stopped on the road below, and someone got out, but no one saw me.

August 11

Today is the day I'm calling home. Either I keep hiking or I don't. I'm now prepared mentally to quit. I walked on the road all the

"...the battle with the chipmunks."

way around. A couple stopped and took a picture, the lady running back with her head down and sweater slapping in the breeze. A few passers-by laughed at my black legs. I guess they were kind of dirty. I had lunch overlooking the lake. The water is incredibly blue. At the shore it turns rainbow colors. A few jays (the kind Bob loved so much) hacked and cawed through my lunch. A ways down I could see Mt. McLoughlin. But no Mt. Shasta. I really didn't like seeing people. I felt conspicuous (which I was), dirty (which I was). I hate seeing people who seem to be headed home the next day or so. I'm really depressed. Will I be home next week? (God, I hope not.) At the Rim Village (no one sees I'm dirty), I walked into the bathroom. I was black. I washed off, guzzled a quart of milk, and sat. Then I saw three people who really did look like long distance hikers. I introduced myself, and we all went up to a ritzy restaurant where I watched them munch salads and hamburgers. Tim Keating — red afro, tall, a little like Bobby;[21] Marie Toombs, a geology professor who was blond, probably forty, still good-looking, and acting like a sixteen-year-old; and Jamie Garrison, who was small, hairy, and who moaned every time the pretty waitress wearing a mini skirt floated by. He was great. I had a blast. Tim said, "Whatever you do, don't quit the hike! Just come north with us, but don't quit!" They all comforted me, gave me some hamburger; we swapped jokes, and Tim fell into a mad reverie on how much he hated Ryback.[22] He'd stare so hard he almost went cross-eyed. Jamie, I found, was infamous for hiking in the nude. They helped so much.

A man gave me a ride to the post office, where I got my birthday cake (fruit cake) and other things, plus a birthday card. Then I called home. Dad just said, "Well, what do you think?" I said, "I think I can do it, but only if y'all are behind me." What a great conversation. I had committed myself for three and a half more months. Then I called Margaret and Randy,[23] and while I was saying "Hi!" I turned and there was Katy right there beside me. I hugged her while yelling over the phone, and then we talked about what had happened to me and about *Dune;* and Margaret said, "Tom, you can't stop now. We're counting on you, you know." I then talked to Katy who had lost Bob. Completely. She was worried, but we caught up on lost times. She was staying with a United States Geological Survey party, and I met a Youth Conservation Corps leader, who let me take a shower in her room (I *was* dirty). I then slept by a tree after walking through the woods for a while to get away from the road. Things could not have gone better. Hallelujah!

> *Now I yearn for one of those old,*
> *meandering, dry, uninhabited roads,*
> *which lead away from towns . . . .*
>
> Henry David Thoreau
> **The Journal of Henry D. Thoreau**

"I'd appreciate it if you'd get up now."

August 12

I awoke to find out I was about ten feet from the highway and in plain view. There was Mr. Ranger looking down at me with his wide-brimmed brown hat. "I'd appreciate it if you'd get up now. I can see you know where you're supposed to be. You're supposed to be at least one mile from a road. You didn't quite make it." I kind of blinked with swollen sleepy eyes and gargled, "OK, sorry," and got up. I got back with Katy eventually, and we talked some more. I can't believe she lost Bob. "We were arguing, and I started walking away, and he was gone." Bob turned up, though. He was at the rim. We had lunch, without Bob, in the survey trailer, and then I hugged Katy 'bye and continued on. I imagine I'll see her in Seiad Valley. Without my asking, a lady stopped and gave me a ride to the trailhead. Earlier that day I had been writing home when a van stopped and out popped two little girls who had batons spinning in their hands.

Anyway, the trail wound easily up, about as wide as a dirt road. I crossed the "Oregon Desert" — a couple of miles of sparse trees and completely flat land. After those encouraging words, it was good to be out. I felt like I was accomplishing something. The idea of being almost halfway helped a lot too. I finally got to my campsite, Stuart Falls, as it was about to get dark. Already there was Alain Vanel from France. It was good to talk to him, and the fire and waterfall were nice. I had tuna and rice, and we talked about hitchiking, food in America, and looked at a map. Eventually I fell asleep under a tree-crossed starry sky.

August 13

Alain Vanel and I had breakfast together. I gave him some powdered milk for his "insta meelk breakfast," and he gave me some matches. I can't believe I forgot to get some in Crater Lake. Alain, you're a lifesaver. We went our separate ways, me ever southward. I kept a good pace back up to the crest to reattain the trail, thinking of Lisa, Gia, and John and all the fun we'd have when I got back.

I hiked slowly, taking too many breaks as usual, pushing for Ranger Springs, my next water supply. I missed the trail to Ranger (with great orientating accuracy), and found myself talking to two girls in their mid-twenties. One had had a stress fracture in southern Oregon and had to lay up for two weeks in Ashland. They told me of northern California, how the trail went up one canyon and down the next. I couldn't wait. I was getting close to that place where two and a half weeks ago I had dreamed of being — near the High Sierra and closer to home. I left and kept on thinking of standing on Whitney, seeing Mexico. My desire for home was so incredibly intense, a tugging I have never felt so strongly before in my life. I dreamed of crying with joy at being near the border. Unimaginable, incomprehensible joy. What could it be like to be home? I felt like I hadn't been there for years.

On the map I carried was an arrow with "water" written in Penny's handwriting, written long ago in that cabin back in the first week of the hike. Of course, there was no water there. I tanked up at a stream nearby and headed for Devil's Peak, an easy hike. Hah. I really blew myself out climbing that thing. I was racing the shadow line of the settling sun as it crept up the opposite ridge. After almost being in tears at not being able to hike well because of fatigue, I attained the top. No great views ahead, just symmetrical bulbs that were tree-covered ancient volcanoes; and looking back I got to see the other side of Crater Lake's rim.

The sun was going fast. I trotted on, cursing the approaching night. I passed over Shale Butte, boots cracking on the broken sharp rock that gave the Butte its name. My feet hurt so bad. I was trying hard to get to Snow Lakes, a supposedly nice camp-site; but like all nice campsites, I missed it. I just didn't see the turnoff and kept right on going as the sun flicked behind the horizon. So I camped on the ridge among some trees. For some reason I felt amazingly vulnerable. The night was completely silent. Not a single sound — the kind of night where a match flame sticks straight up. Thoughts of bears motivated me to build a small fire, and I had dinner in my little hemisphere of light, with complete black and all outdoors just an arm's reach away. The stars were beautiful again.

August 14

Zero water, so no breakfast. I trotted off back to where I missed the trail the night before and at Snow Lakes had a Pop Tart and some instant breakfast. That put me behind. I met an attractive girl sweating her way uphill — then her parents who were close behind. Later I met three women in their sixties standing atop a rock slab and for some reason laughing hysterically. One was a large German-type lady with a German accent who would have made a great general. I said hello; they asked if I was alone and then said be careful. I never knew why they were laughing.

The lakes in this area were beautiful. Deep blue with towering gray rock walls on the other shore. I couldn't pass by without drinking some water out of each. A few mosquitoes kept me from staying long, though. They're not that bad now. After a few confusing forks, I left this lake region and kept on an almost perfectly level, straight two-mile section, with no views. At these times I get so lost in my thoughts that I hardly remember anything at all. I had a late lunch and read some *Dune,* and then continued on over swampy, mosquito infested Horse Creek to Badger Lake. I felt terrible about stopping after only thirteen miles, but I couldn't make myself continue. So I made a lentil dish and nearly finished *Dune.* By then it was pretty dark, and I camped without using my tent. That night a few deer came tromping by, and one of them kept making this loud whooshing sound. It was kind of scary hearing this sound approach from far away, get closer and closer, pass by, and then disappear again. Bear stories prompted me to hang my food.

August 15

Today was the day I was going to make up all the mileage I lost yesterday. I got off to a great start, but I can't seem to be able to get up before the sun. As I was leaving, the birds just started chirping; and I had to rub my hands a little against the chill. I had on shorts and also my wool shirt. So the air was getting slightly chillier. Fourmile Lake was awfully barren. Some of it had been logged, and lots of trunks were floating in the water. Mt. McLoughlin also looked quite stark there. Being late in the season, almost all the snow had melted off it; and it seemed as if the mountain had been stripped naked, as if something was missing. Just kind of light purple volcanic dirt.

I passed by some long-hairs around a bonfire — they took no notice of me, and I began climbing. At the top of the climb I had an unobstructed view of the Klamath Valley below and of the desert lands beyond. After a little reverie I dropped on down over the Cascade Canal and then across a few dirt roads to finally get to Highway 140. Very hungry, I had a good lunch near the highway, though again short of my goal for lunch. I still had thirteen miles to go before camp.

Klunking across the paved highway, I turned onto another road, stepping off to the side to let cars pass. I walked by a resort campground, got some water — again feeling very lonely — and began the long hike down the road. I passed an older couple on their bikes who, after hearing what I was doing, offered me a swim in Lake of the Woods where they had a cabin. I declined. Lord, I can't believe I did that. True, I had to get going, but I hadn't swum yet on this hike. I kept on after many thanks. This road seemed to be a drag strip for logging trucks. I'd trudge along, staring at the straight line of asphalt going all the way out of sight and shimmering in the heat, and a truck loaded with timber would pass by to return again empty. Then another truck would pass in the other direction, again loaded, and would return empty. Someone's organization is screwed. I fancied seeing the same logs being shuttled back and forth.

After passing several ominous NO TRESPASSING signs, I met a hiker, Tom something or other, who had a cowboy hat, bright smile, and long hair which ended in ringlets. I asked him if he had seen where the trail detours off the road. "Haven't you passed it?" he asked. "I don't think so," was my erroneous reply. This was getting embarrassing. After his telling me some about California and exchanging gumdrops for Sunbursts, we continued on. It seemed as if no one has hiked the High Sierra yet, it's so gutted with snow. Everyone I've met has gone around.

I attacked Old Baldy with vigor, looking forward to my first view of Mt. Shasta, and quickly fell into an evil-eyed trudge. This uphill was getting long, and the sun was going fast. Wet with sweat, I came over the knob and there was Shasta. It was beautiful. It and its parasitic cone, Shastina, were streaked with snow. Such a majestic mountain, standing so erect and high. It was caught in alpenglow, and the dusk was again eerily quiet,

"I fancied seeing the same logs being shuttled back and forth."

an early moon crescent suspended above. What a view. I'm actually, finally, seeing California. So, so far away from home. I thought a little about arriving at the California border and continued on down the brushy slopes. I was hiking in almost complete darkness, through some logged areas, when I gave up the chance of reaching my water source and went to sleep after a dry supper of tuna and crackers. I heard some pretty wild sounds that night. I'd hear a few twigs snapping, and I'd clench my teeth, heart racing, and wait for some impending crash or thud; but nothing else would happen. I guess they were squirrels or something.

August 16

I slipped out of sleep and heard a loud sharp squeal. Above me on a tree a few feet away a squirrel was screaming at me, jerking down the side of the tree. Every time I moved, it would squeal and scramble around to the other side, only to come bouncing and screaming back. I had no water, so I gave up my attempts at retreating from the day by crawling deeper into my sleeping bag. Finally I got up and moved on to the ever-distant water source.

I was glad I hadn't gotten there last night, once I did get there this morning, because the water was horrible. It came running down a slope of mud to a cow-mashed and cow-polluted pool of muck. I tried to get some water close to the spring's source, but that also was muddy.

It was cold this morning. I held up my hands to get the sun on them, and after a dry breakfast of a Pop Tart and Space Food Sticks I moved on.

The land was flat and resembled cow pastures, with a few clumps of forest here and there. I crossed a lot of logging roads, and Shasta was always present to my left. I know that seeing that mountain for the first time last night is a view I won't ever forget.

My feet and stomach began hurting soon, and I stopped at Grizzly Creek for a rest and water (finally). Foot scratching and massaging has become a nightly ritual, and if I forget to do it, like last night, my feet rebel.

I passed by Howard Prairie Lake, which the guidebook says is a great place to layover, but I passed it up. I hate doing that, but I have no choice if I'm going to do what I want to do. I was rewarded with a massive uphill, hot and no shade. For some reason I'm so hungry I've been munching all day.

After then paralleling a road for a while I got to the next source, an off-road water spigot which didn't work. I couldn't believe it. Why didn't I tank up at Grizzly Creek? Finally, I dropped down to Hyatt Lake to the campground there and ate what was left of lunch. Bathrooms! I walked in, sat on the toilet just to sit down and be inside, and read some. The day was getting late, however, and I angrily returned to the trail, mad that again I wasn't going to make my twenty miles. I can't do that. I'll have to figure out something.

A man and his kids were trailer camped at Little Hyatt Reservoir, and I smiled, got a drink, and moved on. When I came to a questionable fork at a dirt road, I gave up and made camp. A great camp. I was on a hillock under a tree overlooking Ashland, and the town lights twinkled below. I was nested in tall, brown grass and watched the sun disappear. Earlier that day I had trudged through two cow pastures, and each time the cows slowly took notice of me — and then all of them became my audience as I walked among them. It was neat — all these white faces staring right at you.

But that night I heard a loud snap. Something was tearing the limbs and bark off the tree I was under. Then I heard a slow munching sound, and the thing would then rip off something else. I don't know when I've been so scared. My remedy was to burrow as deep as possible into the sleeping bag, and finally I fell asleep. I never found out what that was.

> *When camping in such a wilderness as this, you are prepared to hear sounds from some of its inhabitants which will give voice to its wildness. Some idea of bears, wolves, or panthers runs in your head naturally, and when this note is first heard very far off at midnight, as you lie with your ear to the ground, — the forest being perfectly still about you, you take it for granted that it is the voice of a wolf or some other wild beast . . .*
>
> Henry David Thoreau,
> **The Maine Woods**

August 17

After some oatmeal and a rare devotion time, I was off. About a hundred yards later I ran into a spigot (I don't know what it was doing there) and tanked up. What followed was just a confused slog through dirt roads and cow herds, following ribbons that bent everywhere and nowhere; and suddenly I ended up on a dirt road, which was the temporary PCT.

I crossed a paved road onto another paved road and began hiking up it, then asked a couple in a passing brown car if they had seen the PCT. I knew I had to have passed the junction. I had apparently, so I walked on up with hopes of catching it where it recrossed the road. After consuming about half a bag of peanut M&Ms, I came to a cabin where there lived a bearded man, wearing rope for a belt, and his German shepherd. He helped a little with directions, and later a guy in a white pickup offered a ride. We talked about cougars and his two dogs, while the latter were yelping in the back. He told me of one dog that had bitten a porcupine and almost died having the quills removed. He departed with a wave, and shortly thereafter I met the trail in a grassy field, going up to the right. I met a man in his thirties who had hiked from Weldon (first one through the High Sierra!). We talked about an hour, and he told me about California. I really can't wait. The deer season has begun; we heard some gunshots. He gave me some mint cake (yum), and we went our ways. I found a trough for a spring with crystal clear water next to a dilapidated cabin. It was in a green field overlooking the valley. A great lunch stop.

I crossed the ridge about ten times, each time opening and closing a gate. Mt. Shasta was still beautiful. Clouds are coming in, which gives great shade. Another nasty water hole from a pipe, but I drank up anyway. It was in a little enclosed area with another dilapidated stable.

My mind is on Callahan's. A troupe of horses were taking their masters for a ride. I attained a flat, high plateau with a great view. The horsy people were on a distant ridge; the sun was beginning to sign off; the clouds were surreal and beautiful; and below was I-5. There was a high wind, too. I loved that place but decided to move on downhill to get to I-5, and then I'd only have three more days to California.

At the end of the dirt road I had a mile to go before camp, at Interstate Five. I then remembered Callahan's. I can't wait. A pickup came up from behind, and I smiled and stuck out my thumb. So what, one mile isn't a big deal. Here's to you, Eric Ryback. It was great to sit in that truck and move again without my legs moving. Just sixty more miles and the five hundred mile Oregon section would be complete! I wonder what the drivers thought seeing me smiling in the back there looking around.

After changing into long pants and shirt behind Callahan's, I walked in with my pack. The place was really nice; people were coming in with long dresses and formal stuff on. I had a blast, though. I ate three bowls of minestrone soup, a salad, the whole basket of crackers, spaghetti, and ice cream, and hors d'oeuvres. I wonder if I'm losing some ability to talk and be around people. I couldn't think of anything to say to the waitress, and I felt really nervous. There were a couple of college-age guys and their dates across the room. I've forgotten that life completely — to be clean, pressed, dry, perfumed, shaven, and combed. I just stared.

Mr. Callahan let me sleep in the front of the restaurant. I had trouble going to sleep, with the cars on the highway, headlights swerving over me, and three dogs that kept sniffing around me. For some reason I felt rotten. I guess when I get a full stomach my mind has a chance to think of other things — like home.

Callahan's to Walker Meadows

August 18

Rain! A good smattering pelted me, and I threw my tent over myself early that morning and awoke to a gray sky. Possibly the first one since the Fourth of July! I had a few cold oatmeals and a Pop Tart, and the sniffing dogs encouraged me to get up and get going. The highway was still in the process of building up to its morning roar. The parking lot was empty, except for one car. Inside rain-streaked windows a couple was sleeping. I felt like I was from another world when I glanced in.

A short hike up an access road to the highway soon put me switchbacking up the side of the valley. The clouds reminded me of days at home when I stayed inside in this weather, and I was enjoying the hike. Higher up the trail I could look back and see the patchwork quilt valley I had just come out of — my last few days' hike, and Shasta still far to the east.

The trail decided to leave me, and for about two hours I pushed through manzanita bushes. It just disappeared. A dirt road led me to a paved one paralleling the "trail" above, so I followed the road, reading *Dune*. The clouds left completely.

The trail popped up across the road, so I struck off following an easy grade and found myself at times in eight-foot high weeds.

It was beautiful though, purple, red, yellow flowers everywhere — my first steps in the Siskiyous, which looked a lot like the Apps.[24] I had lunch at a crystal clear spring — which seemed to be made for drinking, spouting out of the ground across the trail. It felt good to have my short foray into civilization over.

The following eight miles just hugged the ridge, and I walked with the crest just above me and then crossed it at a dip. The grasses and brush were green. At one saddle the wind was high, and I could see a long, long ways. The hike was uneventful, except when towards day's end I spotted a thick column of smoke in the valleys to the north. (Turned out to be a controlled fire.)

With aching, itching feet I finally got to Wrangle shelter about 7:30 P.M. and met about five high school guys and an attractive Youth Conservation Corps leader named Susan — in her late twenties — all with a cooler containing an oversupply of food. We talked awhile. I told them about my hike, and they offered two pork chops. I really liked these people.

Then came Bill and Dave, the Forest Rangers. Bill Roberts was a black-moustached, attractive man who seemed to be a magnet, his personality was so friendly. Dave was quiet and just kind of smiled in the wake Bill made. Bill gave me some ravioli, beans, meatballs, and peanuts, all in one bowl, and then some watermelon. I was stuffed. Two great meals in two days. He talked to the YCC group about their work, told me about the upcoming trail, and put everyone in a great mood. He had a huge dog named Bear. And he said to look out for the Swiss-chalet-styled outhouse described in the guidebook. Turned out it was a sheer rock cliff below a campsite with a great view, but no walls for privacy. I said I'd look for it. But that night I slept by a fire in the shelter surrounded with friendly people. I won't forget that.

August 19

Today is the day. I got a late start, but being there was worth it. The YCC guys were freezing, so they said, and couldn't get up. I guess I've gotten acclimated, because I wasn't cold at all. Even a bit warm. Also, Susan gave me a peach for my Familia. That was delicious.

We said goodbyes, heartfelt ones for me, and I left to go back to the crest. I also had given Susan my book, *Dune;* she had always wanted to read it.

I followed almost exactly the contour of the ridge, and I kept craning my neck over the next ridge, for I knew California was just over there. My feelings of disbelief kept me from being really excited, and also the fact that California wasn't that much different. I guess I expected cliffs and red deserts or something.

But I slogged down a logged out area and then saw a little wooden sign tacked to a tree that said CALIFORNIA. That was it. Not even an Oregon sign on the other side of the tree. On the ground was a large note — staked there by the three I had met in Crater Lake — that said: THE CALIFORNIA-OREGON BORDER OF THE PACIFIC CREST TRAIL. TAKE A DUMP IN CALIFORNIA, I'M ALRY-GONE IN OREGON. REVOLVING RAMEN CLAIMS THIS AS THE OFFICIAL BORDER, among other things. After an M&M break — my homage to the border — I went on down into a beautiful glade with swampy weeds waist high and then began climbing.

I had my first California lunch at an intersection of five dirt roads. The map looked like spaghetti. Two guys who said they were looking for some place to go "huntin' for gold" drove up. I tried to help them get oriented and then took off, climbing past several springs to the top of the crest, and again Mt. Shasta rose to greet me. I was almost directly west of it now. It's neat to get a view of each side as I swing around it. But I thought of the time ahead, of living three more months out here like this. Six months is indeed a long, long time.

I checked out Alex Hole Camp with its Swiss chalet outhouse. I paid homage to it as well, in my own way. And the view was good. An appropriate name. After meandering among some slow, wary cows I got some water from the spring's source and went back to the trail. I hate cows. They always pollute the water.

I then made camp — a beautiful one, or at least homey, with a large bonfire right under an ABSOLUTELY NO CAMPFIRES sign. The fire made the tree waver, and it gave me kind of an eerie feeling.

Earlier that day on the trail I had crossed an area of silicon and had walked on shimmering shards of rock. Also, the bees are becoming plentiful down here.

August 20

After a breakfast of Jell-O and some rancid dried fruit, I began to walk the last few maps of volume two of the guide book. Seiad Valley is ahead. A new set of maps, clothes, some books! some food — all await my arrival. I was very excited.

I made good time that morning. Over a few buttes with few breaks. I spotted a tiny stake that had WATER printed on it and descended to a cool spring. Ahead I could follow the trail all the way to the last visible ridge, where it then dropped into Seiad Valley. A big drop. From six thousand to seventeen hundred feet. There were Red Butte, Kangaroo Mountain, and the three Devils peaks — erect, steepsided, brushy mountains, all living up to their own namesakes.

I descended on towards Cook and Green Pass. Whistling and rounding a corner, I could hear some rustling and breaking of twigs. A deer, I thought.

It was a bear.

A big black bear, twenty feet from me. I froze. I couldn't do anything. My heart was about to jump up my throat. The bear took little notice of me, and he slowly turned his head in my direction. He was tearing up a tree, his feet wrapped around the trunk, his back to me. He saw me, blinked, rose up on his haunches, and dove down the slope, his body shaking and swerving as he ran; and then all I could see was dust and the tops of little trees come wrenching down, and all I could hear was a sound like thunder or a freight train. The ground shook.

I straightened up when he was gone. My first bear. I couldn't believe it. I was finally seeing a bear close up! I whistled loudly from then on so as not to have another surprise encounter.

After lunch at hot Cook and Green Pass, I started on a short cut down a dirt road. The sun was blazing hot and the no-see-ums bothersome. But I passed a few waterfalls, and the trail was easily followed. I was worn out, though. Forty-five miles in the past two days had gotten to me. The walk down was uneventful but nice; for one of the first times of the hike the mountains rose around me, the trees clustered, and the sound of the Seiad Creek was flowing up from the valley depths. This place reminded me of the farm.

I stopped there at the river to look at a beautiful waterfall and swimming hole and wanted to swim in it, but instead I just had some tea and then pushed on. Eventually the dirt road became paved. The walk was neat . . . . Lining the road were several homes, most with a television playing in some unseen room, and all with a run-down car in the yard. Not a person to be seen. Like a ghost town. I walked the paved road for a couple miles with my feet killing me. A rambling, banging pickup hurtled by. I stuck out my thumb for a second and instantly got a ride. One more mile to Seiad; I really don't care. The town was also deserted, displaying a big banner across the main street with Mark Twain Festival on it. A few water sprinklers spritzed a kind hello.

At a trailer park, I walked along on the green grass there. A man saw me and said, "They're waiting for you."

Huh?

There were Katy and Bob. We hugged, said hello, talked. Katy's great. Bob and I still have a wall between us, though we speak. But it's so nice to talk to someone. Katy said I was emaciated. She and Bob both looked incredibly healthy. Seems they've had a blast these past couple of weeks. I ate a complete gummy failure of noodles for dinner and went on to sleep. Katy and Bob were lying close together, laughing and whispering. That sound was beautiful, though I felt a little like the third person. The stars are great.

August 21

This day I did absolutely nothing. Walking hurts a little, which scares me, but after a while I felt a little better. Man! Massive quantities of everything at the post office. Food, books, clothes! And of course, the letters, the most treasured items. Katy had just received a box from her mom, which contained, above the food she needed, about thirty quarts worth of powdered milk. "My mom must have gone crazy," she laughed. I washed and dried, and mostly pored over the new California maps while eating cheese straws. Bill, the ranger, had left five bucks at the P.O. for me, to celebrate my entry to California. What a great guy. I had a banana-pineapple milkshake and then went by to see him at the ranger station. What a bright-eyed, funny guy. He just envelops you when you talk to him. Quiet Dave was there, too. He gave me the PCT emblem blaze. I'll treasure that. A note from Penny and Bill! They'll be here tomorrow! Man, I can't wait to see those guys. It was great to do nothing. The heat is incredible.

I planned out all the drops ahead up to Tuolumne. It seems so short. As always, the call home was refreshing. Some yahoos kept revving down the main street on motorcycles, so talking was difficult but great. We decided on a camera. They're going to send one!

August 22

I had a nice breakfast at the cafe with Bill's present. Pancakes, eggs, bacon, toast. The cook was an easygoing man with white apron who would just sit around, eyes half open, with a paper in his hand, and some jerky morning variety show played on a little television set. Someone I faintly remembered was singing some song I faintly remember. That world of clean and glittery white I've forgotten completely. I really can't remember what it's like.

I had a trail lunch to save money. Three north-bounders walked into town. One of them said, "Hey! You walk the whole way?" I said, "Yeah . . . except for St. Helens . . . ." He withdrew his extended hand, which kind of made me mad. But they're all right, and they've certainly accomplished a lot. One guy's shirt jumped, and a little kitten poked its head from between two buttons. Found on the trail.

One of the trio had the hike down to an art. He opened his box from the P.O. and pulled out sealed plastic packets with complete proportioned meals with vitamin packs. I couldn't be that organized. We exchanged trail information while they devoured egg sandwiches and a half-gallon of ice cream. Then they said they had seen Penny and Bill! A little black-haired girl and a tall, lanky blond guy? Yep.

I must have gotten the notes screwed up. They were ahead of me. I hugged Katy goodbye and shook Bob's hand; they were on their way home. About 3:00 P.M. I finally got started. Visiting with them again was so great. Bob and I may never understand each other, but Katy will always be remembered. I said goodbye to the three north-bounders and took off. I wanted to embrace

"...a little kitten poked its head from between two buttons."

the entire town and thank everyone for all the hospitality and friendship. But the town just sat, and everyone was still there and would always be there doing what they do. I turned down the road.

But Seiad was not through with me yet. A husky, Robert Redford-looking chap stopped while I was enmeshed in a thicket of blackberries and invited me to his house for dinner. We put my pack on a precarious place on his trailer and took off. Dennis, his wife, son, and friends welcomed me to their home and served me a large portion of some incredible spaghetti. As always happens when people become interested in the hike, he began handing me pamphlets and books I could take with me. His friend was huge, obese, bearded, and hilarious. We went fly-fishing, which I artfully fumbled. Tim (the friend) kept getting the line caught up with Dennis's dog. It was a blast. The friend came up to me that night and handed me his favorite lure, with a touch of reverence. "When all else fails, this one will catch anything." A perfect evening, when I was displaced back into civilization, company, and a little of home.

Dennis gave me a ride back to the trail with his wife and son, and we talked of coyotes. He would look out the window with a slight smile and would say to his son, "Just think, tomorrow Tom will be a little further south, the next day a little further, and in four months at the border." It sounded good to hear someone say that. A brilliantly moonlit night. I said goodbye to Dennis the trapper and his son and quickly went to sleep next to bubbling Grider Creek.

August 23

I had breakfast-in-bag and started from Seiad Valley up Grider Creek. Soon I encountered a box for getting permits for the Marble Mountain Wilderness. I looked inside — and there was one for Peter Wirth dated ten days ago! Good night, he moves fast. Maybe I can catch him yet. And here was one for "Revolving Ramen," too. I guess they came through a long time ago.

The hike up was beautiful. There were colored leaves on the trail, some at least, and thoughts of Thanksgiving and Christmas began to sift through my head. The trail went up moderately, and the sun was hitting the other side of the canyon, so I was nice and cool. The creek (or "crick," as locals in Seiad call it) was beautiful. It rushed and bubbled through marble troughs and boulders. So much creamy white marble down there where the soil was washed away. I imagined Michelangelo would have had a heyday here. No time to fish, though.

And there was quiet Dave, fishing away. "Yeah . . . heh, heh, haven't caught anything yet, heh,heh, but, heh, you know, heh, heh . . . ." There was a friend across the creek plowing through the shrubbery.

The trail continued up and up. Not until later did I realize this was one of the longest climbs of the hike. I began to take it in steps, and as I moved up I could see across the valley to the mountains that I had walked on three days before.

I stopped for a breather, and a curious, nervous, solitary horse kept tramping around. I got a little nervous too and pushed on 'til I met a hiker. Only after fifteen minutes of conversation, while he inspected his much-bandaged toes, did he tell me it was his birthday. I handed him some M&Ms as a present. He promised easy trails ahead, and I promised him the same as he descended into Seiad. I was out of dense forest and was pondering whether a trail could go uphill forever when it leveled off. Through a patch of crackly dried grass I found a deep, cool spring. After loading up I then spied a hiker under a low shady tree. Even though the sun was dipping low, I decided to go on after a couple of minutes of talking. He was quiet and gazed off in the distance quite a bit. So I figured he wanted to be alone. He had been on the trail for five months.

It was a mistake to push on. I was on Big Ridge, hoping to get to Paradise Lake, when the sun disappeared. My aching feet convinced me to stop at a gap in the ridge next to a post. Nothing on it, just a post stuck on the top of this ridge. The grass was stubby and fairly comfy. The wind died down after my dry supper of crackers and tuna. The ensuing silence was awesome. I had to break it with another try at "Oh Susanna" and "Silent Night" on the harmonica. The stars are beautiful, and the silence makes them more so. I put up the harmonica in my pack, which was against the post at my head, and went to sleep.

August 24

I caught the first rays of the sun on the ridge and started off in search of water. It was a long time coming. The sun is hot and the trail at times dusty and rocky. I could hear streams down the ridge side, but as always, the brilliant trail engineers directed

Callahan's to Walker Meadows/99

the trail up and away from water. I finally caught up with a gurgling stream rolling through some tall rushes. It's a very clear, hot day. After a late breakfast of oatmeal and instant breakfast, I kept on. An older man and woman greeted me next to Paradise Lake. The lake is nestled under Kings Castle, a sloping wall with a surface of short grass and rock. The trail kept getting harder to follow as it meandered through tall grasses, but I followed the ridge and stayed on it. The trail topped ridge after ridge, with water always splashing out of sight down the slope.

I met a long-haired hiker with a cowboy hat who warned me of hard trails ahead — no water, no scenery, sometimes no trail. But he told me of the old granny ranger at Grizzly Peak Lookout who supplies water and an hour or so of companionship playing cards. Looking forward to meeting the Grizzly Peak Granny, I moved on down into a valley where I met two more hikers. I had to be near a road.

But no, they're hiking from Mexico. The guy seemed pretty upset. "You know what PCT stands for?" he asked. "Pretty Crummy Trail." The female side of the couple was smiling away, despite a knee brace and ace bandages on each leg. Her T-shirt read "Canada or breast boob bust," with breast and boob crossed out. I wonder if they'll make it.

I finally hit the valley bottom. It sported a muddy trickle of a stream and a locked up guard station — and a note from Penny and Bill. They had left, had gone off the trail to skip to the High Sierra, leaving some maps and a note under a rock. A guy eating lunch there said they had left just that morning. This is the third time I've missed them!

After a lunch embellished with Space Food Sticks (thank you, Mom!), I started up the other valley wall. The terrain is very brushy and covered with trees. The world's deepest caves reside here. Before lunch I explored a marble cave, which wasn't deep or high, but it had beautiful fluted marble stalactites. Like the wall of a cathedral.

The climb was long, but the view at the top was windy and beautiful. The eastern section of the Marble Mountain Wilderness is composed of steep knife-edged ridges covered with grass and the last wildflowers of the summer.

I walked the ridge, weaving in and out between peaks, and each view cradled a lake, now a soft deep blue due to the approaching dusk. The ridge drops off sharply at times on both sides of the trail. I met an elfish looking man, smiling under a huge brimmed hat, with shiny, tiny eyes, and flanked on each side by a young girl — the three of them drinking grape juice. "So you're hiking that Pacific Coast Trail." He wouldn't believe it was the Pacific Crest Trail.

Although the sunset was gorgeous, the trail downhill, and scenery everywhere, my spirits hit a low. Just rushing through this land killing myself made me cry. I yelled and cried and cried and yelled. It felt great and was enough to make me stop way short of my goal. I got some water in the last light of the day from a trickling spring ensuing somewhere from a huge granite cliff. I built a fire in the dark and, enclosed in my own personal home of light, ate one of the best meals of the hike. Some bacon grease that Dennis from Seiad had given me made the noodles incredible. I read some of C.S. Lewis.[25]

The night was also one of the most magical of the entire hike. The moon still gilded every contour of the land in silver. The granite cliff with its rocky lap upon which I was camped was shimmering. I love the moon. It's a clock, slowly and reassuringly marking each month. What a friend. I thought of little Crater Lake back in northern Oregon, the last time I had seen this moon.

After I was asleep the deer came out. I awoke several times to loud whuffing sounds of the deer blasting air through their nostrils. If I moved, their hooves would crack against the rock as they ran. Sounded like gunshots. Just so they knew I was there, I didn't care.

And I forgot to say that after I reached
the road by Potter's bars, — or further,
by Potter's Brook, — I saw the moon
suddenly reflected full from a pool. A
puddle from which you may see the moon
reflected, and the earth dissolved under
your feet. The magical moon with atten-
dant stars suddenly looking up with mild
lustre from a window in the dark earth.

Henry David Thoreau
The Journal of Henry D. Thoreau

August 25

[P.S. I saw a bear the day before yesterday, way across the valley.
Apparently I had scared him, and he was scampering away into
some trees.] I got a late start today. A brilliantly blazing sun made
it necessary to squint to look up at all. The trail bounced up and
down through volcanic, sponge-looking rock. I met a shirtless,
athletic looking hiker with dark glasses striding up the hill. Even
though he had come from Weldon, he showed no signs of a long
hike, no hunched shoulders or thin torso. We talked for about
fifteen minutes, and he told me about the Hat Creek Rim. "It's
incredibly bad. Two guys got dysentery by drinking some water
there. Piss on the Rim."

With these encouraging words of northern California, I dropped on down where the trail began to flatten out as it contoured
the top of the ridge almost perfectly. Another hiker: this guy's
walking every step from Mexico. He's shirtless, has on tennis
shoes, and his thin shoulders hunched forward over a hollow
chest. I hope that doesn't happen to me. He was kind of Orien-
tal looking and was one of those people who don't seem to be
able to swallow their saliva; his mouth sputtered and bubbled
when he talked. We didn't say much; he took a picture while
I ate a chocolate bar. Really a pleasant person. He showed me
some of his highlighted maps, complained about southern California, and we departed. That familiar pit in my stomach began

to form, telling me the day was fleeting while I had gotten nowhere.

A beautiful view of Shelly Fork valley popped up, and I kept on going on a completely new stretch of trail. There was a lone house in an alpine meadow next to the trail, and the marshy, tepid water I got there warranted a couple of purification tablets. My map warned "Last Water to Paynes Lake" sixteen miles away. The trail was very even and not at all difficult to trod. It had been balanced on three steep ridges, and I could follow ten miles of trail with my eye as I looked ahead. Red rock, sparse pine, and an abundance of manzanita bushes were ahead.

The hike was long and uneventful. My water disappeared, my feet tired, and rest stops became more frequent. Wow! my first rattlesnake! It was beheaded, small, and without tail — not much for story telling, but made me more wary of them.

The line between shadow and the last red rays of sun kept working its way up the side of the ridge. I crossed a dirt road at a gap next to a concrete block — a shed of some kind. No water faucet. I deeply wished someone would drive by.

But no distant rattle of an approaching vehicle came, and I started back on the trail. It was an eerie time of dusk, when it seemed as if some unknown source of light was filtering in from somewhere, and every object was smoky and misty.

I was really thirsty and pounded up the next mountain sweating hard, my lungs and heart pumping in rhythm. But I was getting upset again. I saw I was following a doe, which finally turned and darted away. At the next top of the ridge, I stopped once more and decided to leave the trail and look for water. The moon was going strong now, and distant ridges were milky shadows.

I started down the other side, which was incredibly steep and almost trailless. The first of a series of slips sent me whomping

Callahan's to Walker Meadows/103

down on my rear. That kind of fall seems to yank my emotions out, and the rest of the descent was mixed with yelling and crying and cursing.

The ground began to level out, and I was just walking between trees. All light was gone. But I ran into a clearing and sure enough, there was little Ruffey Lake.

No restraints tonight. I built a big, blazing fire, tanked up with water, and had a large supper (lentils). Once I began drinking I couldn't stop, and I put away three quarts that night. I kept hearing little crackling, skittering noises as some unknown creatures romped around. Their sounds are greatly magnified when it's so quiet and dark. But my harmonica put away the spooky feelings, and I went to sleep.

August 26

I had a very pleasurable morning. After oatmeal and Pop Tarts I walked over to a shelf of rock by the lake. It was flat and warm, so I rinsed off my feet, legs, and arms and slowly dressed again. That felt great. My skin tingles as it dries, even without having used soap.

Deep, dark thoughts about why in the world I was doing this ensued as I reattained the trail.

The trail was gentle, weaving in and out between peaks over broken, crushed rock. Some voices filtered up from one basin, but I couldn't see anyone. I thought of my family. What precious thoughts. It was as if they had died or had never existed except in my head. For my thoughts about them were the same as daydreamy thoughts about anything that hasn't happened or doesn't exist; I could pull out a letter, a concrete object, but it was so small a piece. I honestly couldn't remember what it was like to be with them.

Spasms went through my whole body — a
vague infinite appreciation of the terrible
fact that the past is gone, gone forever!
And with this feeling a vivid panorama of
my life at home moved before my mind.

N. C. Wyeth, **The Wyeths**

The sky was a quiet and seamless blue. The air was a little cool too. I dreamed I was on the beginning of the hike as I walked, and at the top of the next basin I turned to wave goodbye to Mom and Dad, who I imagined were standing down there below on the trail.

The trail was almost an expectant quiet, as if something was about to happen. I thought of painting, sang songs, the same ones for the thousandth time, and at lunch I pulled out the old physics notes for the first time. It didn't seem hard.

The trail topped out on a ridge, revealing one of the most beautiful valleys so far on the hike, Russian Creek valley. The valley was flanked on either side by turrets of white stone, and huge teetering pinnacles rose above me on the ridge. It seemed as if nothing but a string suspended these boulders on their narrow bases, but they had survived many storms and were secure. Each slope was blanketed by a profusion of bright green manzanita bushes for almost two miles down the valley. Far below, the green gave way to a dark blue green on the valley bottom, and a shimmering ribbon of a stream wound down the floor. It looked very much like the Cascades with its steep but smooth bowl shape — the best sight in the Klamath Mountains so far.

It was unusual to find myself still in low spirits. The sun was the same as on a Sunday after church when I would be doing homework or drawing. Again I asked myself, what in heaven's name am I doing here? Across the valley was an ominous black knife of a cliff slicing out from the valley slope and rising above my head. It seemed not to belong in this serene valley. I felt a little camaraderie with something else that seemed out of place.

Water was abundant, and up the trail came three hikers - an old man and a middle-aged couple. They urged not trying to hike far, just to have a good time; don't try to be superman. I guess I needed that.

My spirits warranted a stop, so I camped early on the other end of the valley and began to write Neale. Two more hikers passed by, a young guy and girl. They had that well-worn, sunburned look of long-distance hikers, and indeed they were. They were very tired, but being waterless they had to push on. For me, water had been plentiful today. The wind was picking up, and the air turned much chillier.

> *Our thoughts are the epochs of our life:*
> *all else is but as a journal of the winds*
> *that blew while we were here.*
> Henry David Thoreau
> **The Journal of Henry D. Thoreau**

August 27

Another lone day. I walked on through typical northern California landscape, with mountains giving way to rolling, almost smooth land on either side. Green, green, green.

The birds here are great. They fly in a straight line, high above the ground, and yet when going over a ridge they only barely clear the ridge and so come whizzing by at about ankle height.

A road with a large Forest Service sign: I had entered the Salmon-Trinity Alps. I thought of eating pizza with Stacy and J, of coming back here with my son some day; and I stopped for lunch at a nice stream.

Raspberries abounded here, so I had some tangy, lip-puckering little hard ones (no mature berries) and continued on. Water was abundant, but so were the cowbells, and as I looked up I could see several herds above me. Looks like this is cow country. I felt like I was in Texas with the red-brown earth on the ridge tops Actually that color signifies a volcanic landscape, and the rocks were little sponge textured chunks of purple and red.

The trail ridge traversed for a while, hugging the side of the ridge and poking in and out between peaks. Penny had written that there was a cabin below (with a Monopoly board!), but for lack of competition I decided to stay up and keep going. The trail was very dubious here. Rotten granite had washed away parts, forcing a boulder hop over areas, and at times creating a sand slide which filled boots to the brim. At a fork in the trail there appeared a little paper sign from one hiker to another: "We went from Sec. 32 to Sec. 28 on map P10." The sign looked pretty worn, so they had passed by several days ago.

Although I had been told water was not to be had until Mosquito Lake, I found it in abundance. I skirted Eagle Peak and entered several beautiful meadows of deep green and white cliffs. After slowly dipping water from a stream, cup by cup, I made camp by a tree. Another record fire; lentils again for dinner.

Later that night I heard my friends the coyotes. They were in a frenzy: not mournful yipping, but a crazed chorus of yelps and barks, like hysterical laughter. Cowbells also sounded, so maybe a herd of cattle was being terrorized by coyotes. I rested a little uneasily, thinking of a cattle stampede through my meadow.

August 28

A beautiful morning carried me past Mosquito Lake and Marshy lakes. Red and purple spongy-looking rock — definitely volcanic — and myriads of streams characterized this area. A doe below was taking advantage of the water. I climbed into more forested areas and, during a rest break, scanned the guidebook. Such a long, long way to go. On and on and on. I guess I can say I'm past halfway; I don't know. I had a very hard time getting motivation to keep going.

I celebrated entering the Shasta-Trinity National Forest with lunch at Whiskey-Town Callahan road. This is where all the horror stories of northern California begin. I planned to go around the first stretch of bushwacking by following the road and taking logging roads back to the trail.

During lunch, as I competed with yellowjackets for my pudding, two deer and a grouse came within twenty feet of me. I'm getting to be a champion bee killer. Between mashes and swats, I watched the two does nibble on some leaves and then get antsy and spring away.

The hike down the road provided instant civilization. Suddenly Rovers and jeeps roared by, encasing smiling, bearded faces. Although just behind a car window, those faces were a world away. I was happy to hit the logging roads.

I think. A water truck baptized my boots with water as it passed and turned the road into mud. After checking and rechecking the map several times, I decided to move off onto an overgrown road which headed more north. I questioned this move more and more as it became more overgrown. What bothered me were the non-existent comforting footprints of some other hiker, just to let me know someone had been here before.

The "road" continued up at a steep angle, and bushes began creating a wall, so that I was literally pushing hard to get myself and pack through. These bushes sported red berries. Great! The taste of one berry necessitated a few good gulps of Gatorade and a hard candy. Yech.

I was rewarded at the ridge top with the clank of tractors and roar of hydraulic lifts. The same dirt road I had passed before met me again, and its dusty sides sucked me in shin deep. I was having enough of this. I hopped down the opposite slope over fallen trees to the heart of the logging rumble. Some guy with black beard and hair told me the trail continued on down that road, a report which was confirmed by a pick-up full of fat, red-faced men in overalls.

At Masterson Meadow finally, I figured I could pick up the trail. A quick foot check revealed a little disaster though. I could lift my purple-black toenail clean off my toe. The old guy had held on for a long time (he had begun to turn color at Crater Lake) and was now gone.

A couple of watermelons chilling in the stream by the meadow tempted a short uninvited stay, but my morals got the best of me. That meadow was all swamp, and after mushing around for a while following logging blazes, I finally found a trail blaze.

Past a series of meadows, following nothing but my nose and some miniscule ribbons and ducks, and past several herds of cattle, I got to the trail, or to a trail. Light began to fail, so I looked for a while for a flat spot amid the herd of bellowing cattle I had just scattered. No flat places, not even the trail. I more or less curled around a tree and had a fire on the slope. To top the day off, I put about three times more sauce than needed over some noodles; I threw it out. I went for a backpacking first and cooked chocolate pudding. It came out fine, but I couldn't wait for it to cool, so I drank it on down. The sunset was spectacular.

August 29

My birthday! This day is special. The morning was windy and cloudy — the first clouds since Mt. Rainier back in July. I heard some roaring around the next hill, and lo! the trail builders were at work. I only saw one man there mixing something. He had

"If you're goin' to Mexico, go that way."

next to him a huge red-eyed German shepherd. I got mixed up on the direction, and he had to tell me twice which way to go. "If you're goin' to Mexico, go that way." He jabbed the direction with his thumb.

The trail was new, a virtual sidewalk as it made a slightly inclining line up a manzanita-covered slope. The bushes, being knee high, offered little screening when I stopped to relieve myself. But I guess the trail workers wouldn't care anyway.

At a ledge facing a pass the view spread out, and I could see the valley where I was to follow a trail that a past hiker had marked "indistinct" in the guidebook. Upon descending to Bull

Lake, the trail disappeared altogether. At least I knew it descended, so under an increasingly cloudy sky I waded through thick grass and boulder hopped on down. An occasional blaze let me know I was headed right, and I finally picked up the trail again.

My birthday lunch consisted of the same old peanut butter and honey, but I got to open the freeze-dried vanilla ice cream as well.

After a little reading of *Mere Christianity,* and after some philosophical thoughts about being twenty, I descended onto a dirt road and quickly crossed a stream to start up the other side of the valley. I was enjoying this. It was nice to have a challenge, a thought provoking occurrence. The trail had disappeared again, and I pretended to be a great pathfinder as I worked my way up, sometimes through stream beds, sometimes across marshes or meadows, but never on a trail. I knew a fork was ahead, and when I thought I had gone too far, I pulled out the map, only to find a faint fork ten feet ahead. Apparently cattle knew the trail better than I, for they had trampled a stretch for me. A pattering of rain rose and disappeared. My pack cover was on again — the first time since Washington.

The trail hit a steep hill, up and up, until I thought it wouldn't end. The wind picked up, and there was the gap that was to get me out of this trailless valley.

I walked on to the sandy gap and discovered my destination for this section, Castle Crags. The clouds had split just above them, bathing them in a bright yellow light. Dominating the scene, the spiked and jagged concrete mountain looked like a far away but clearly defined castle. The clouds were dark, the wind still high, and the effect was dramatic.

I switchbacked down the steep slope and at Toad Lake made camp finally. This is my birthday dinner, so no holds barred. I had lentils and, for dessert, demolished the package of s'mores Momma had fixed up. I decided to set the tent up in case of rain. I haven't used this old friend in a while, not since Crater Lake. Across the lake I could hear a few people talking and a radio going, but I decided against walking around to say hello. I don't know why. I wrote Liza White and then went on to sleep. My toe hurts some, but it isn't that bad.

August 30

I got around the lake and started up the next slope by the time those across the lake had awakened and gotten their radio started. The clouds had rinsed the sky clear, and now it was a windy, bright blue. At the ridgetop, Mt. Shasta came into view again, huge and majestic. For some reason I hadn't seen her for awhile, and now as I looked, I realized I was completing the arc around her and was seeing the back side. The first time I had seen her was the evening on Old Baldy in Oregon, and now I had gone all the way around her.

The trail descended through a forested rocky basin and again began ridge topping. Where my map had H₂O AVAILABLE scrawled on it, only a mud spring presented itself — totally unpalatable, unless I were to dig for a while.

I met more trailworkers and, after talking about five minutes, continued on. Apparently they hadn't seen many hikers, for when I answered the question, "Where are you hiking from?" with "Canada," one of the worker's eyes lit up as he exclaimed, "Canada!" First time that's happened, as far as I can remember.

The trail was well marked and easy going but waterless. Many lakes winked at me from far below but were inaccessible. This forced a dry lunch, and I kept on going. I passed some guy jogging (jogging?) with a dog, so I figured I had to be near a road.

The trail forked to hit a perfect contour along a ridge over Seven Lakes Basin. Across the valley was Echo Lake, and suspended above it was gray, dark Boulder Peak. The view was beautiful. I think I sang every single song I've ever known as I continued, the trail leading me to gaps between peaks where I gazed out over more basins and valleys. One notable view was the Devil's Pocket, a steep, rock-faced canyon. I had trouble getting myself going after I stopped to rest. I dropped my pack for the thousandth time, and for the thousandth time felt a cool breeze on my sweat-soaked back, while my shoulders lifted as if in zero gravity. To put that thing back on was the last thing I desired, especially to have to adjust my shirt, pants, and underwear over and over to keep the belt from cutting into my hips.

I decided to take a shortcut, and indeed, the guidebook suggested it. Where the trail made a wide arc around a basin, I could drop two thousand feet down to a logging road and follow that out to Castella, only eight miles away. The map suggested a forested, easy descent, and so it was for about a mile and five hundred feet down. It was kind of nice to be hiking without a trail and to have a secure feeling of knowing I wouldn't get lost. I had only to go down.

I couldn't believe it. I found another trail not even on the map, but this one petered out quickly.

Then came the manzanitas. I found a wonderful little waterfall where I had my first good draught of the day, but the ensuing hike was horrible. The water suggested I was too far north, and heading south was practically impossible. But head south I did. I grunted and scraped and squeezed for two hours through those bushes. Their limbs were resilient enough not to break, but strong enough to catch hold of anything, anything at all — hair, socks, pack; and the bark was slick, so that one couldn't easily walk on the trunks.

It had to be four hours — no, ten hours — that I pushed through there. My sweaty, panting grunts became curses as time passed, and then I was yelling at the top of my lungs to get rid of frustration. I had to fight like crazy to get two feet ahead. A small clump of trees provided a brief respite, but I had to plunge right back in. I yelled and screamed my way on down, at times letting gravity do the work, never being able to touch ground, scrambling just to keep my head above my feet, while branches grabbed and tore and scratched. A queer sight I must have been when the last bush plopped me onto a dirt road with my legs scratched to pieces and twigs and leaves sticking in and out of everywhere.

The "road" I was on was a tail-end in the maze of roads that followed, all of them steep, overgrown, with huge mounds of dirt; but after a time I descended upon what seemed to be a used one. It was getting dark. A splashing stream invited me to stay, and the ends of boards scattered around made excellent firewood. I really cleaned that dirt road up as I made dinner and used every bit of wood available. I read by the light of the fire until the temperature dropped, and then I contentedly, thankfully, crawled into my sleeping bag.

August 31

A beautiful day led me down that old winding dirt road. I could see other logging roads on distant, bright-green hills. The sky was a wistful blue; the sunlight reminded me of an early morning on the farm. As I descended into the clusters of valleys under these hills, I thought of the High Sierra and how close I'll be to finishing when I get to Weldon. Weldon! I can't wait to get there.

I finally reached the main dirt road leading to Castella. I had hardly moved a quarter mile before someone pulled up beside me in a pickup and said, "Want a ride?" Only a few more miles to Castella, all of it road, so why not? I hopped in, feeling a little guilty, but happy for the ride nevertheless.

Man, the guy was driving fast! We whipped around turns, my pack and myself being bounced and shaken and bumped around.

There was a girl hiker ahead, and he pulled up and asked her if she needed a ride; she hopped in.

I'll never forget this horrible feeling, for as I looked at my pack, I could see that my tent was gone. I knocked on the roof of the cab; he stopped, and I jumped out, thanked him, and began the search back up the road. No trail, manzanita bushes, and now this; someone didn't want me to get to Castella. But I knew I'd find my tent. I *had* to.

But a mountain man and his family gave me a ride back up the road in an old black pickup. I searched everywhere, my eyes poking in every corner of the road. I talked the kids in the back into looking too, but they quickly lost interest. We passed the spot where I met the road, but still no tent. I was getting worried.

The mountain man stopped for me to get out, and I began walking back down the road again, weaving from side to side as the realization of no tent began to grow on me. With growing desperation I stopped everyone coming uphill, but no one had seen a tent bag. Some smiled with a "hurts, doesn't it?" or a "this weather is great, you don't need a tent." (That one made me mad.) And others drove slowly past, looking out the window for it. I remember one van crammed full with people my age — the girls were beautiful, and no one had seen a tent bag. The drop off to the right of the road was bushy and steep, about a five hundred-foot drop. The gnawing feeling that it may be just behind that next rock tore and fought with the feeling that I wanted and needed to get to Castella. I could search for weeks and find nothing, or the next step I could find it.

I began to cry as that same helpless, childlike, lost feeling enveloped me. If God doesn't want me to continue, why doesn't he just make me break my leg or something? This is the worst thing that could have happened that still didn't stop the hike definitely. Why does God allow these things to happen? Things that sting so deep; I'm still thinking of how much this trip costs, and now the tent is gone. The monetary loss is very small, but how important that tent is to me, and how difficult it will be to tell Mom and Dad that I no longer have one.... I just can't believe it.

These thoughts ran through my head as I walked the last few steps. It was late afternoon, and I hadn't had lunch, so I was looking forward to getting to Castella. My search had been interrupted for about ten minutes by a foray into a thicket of blackberries, and now I was really hungry.

A brown van took me to the store, where I bought a half-gallon of fudge-ripple ice cream and a can of tomatoes. I settled down on the grass in front, ate, and read some and thought about what had happened with a quieter mind and a full stomach. The heat is great down here. Whew. After reading some *Mere Christiantity* and eating a little more, the light began to fail, and I called home. Apparently I didn't sound very happy — the loss of the tent and the loss of the toenail and the possibility of infection all made the conversation difficult. Also, this place is really gross. I slept behind the post office, next to a parking lot, by the Dempster Dumpsters.[26] Earlier today some long-haired bearded guy in sunglasses had come up to me in the store's restroom. "Wow, man, the PCT, huh? I've worked on that."

"Really?" I said. I guess I sounded like I didn't believe him, because he shot back, "You don't believe me? I've got stuff in my car—wanna see it?"

"No thanks...but I believe you."

"Well, keep cool man, far out."

Yes, I'm definitely in California.

September 1

A new month! I love it. Calling Gaye last night was a big help.

Everyone seems to want to hear about the bear near Seiad. I bought my food for the next section, which wasn't much, since I had a lot left over.

I tried to get to Dunsmuir but wasn't willing to try to hitch on the highway. I *hate* hitchhiking, begging for a ride; I *hate* it! So I came on back, ate about three bologna sandwiches at Sam's Grocery Store, and began to take my leave. Oh yeah! Mom sent a box with pictures of the family and the new baby! plus food. Sam was helpful but uninformed about the trail.

This was to be the rotten section: mostly incomplete, no views, and no water.

I finally got a start, crossed the Sacramento River on a foot bridge, passed by people gathering the profusion of blackberries that hung on the bushes, and I finally came back to the trail. It wasn't inviting, just a dirt trough slicing straight up a hill with no switchbacks. So I sweated on up with intense heat and a horde of tiny black flies that hovered directly in front of my eyes, as if suspended there by an invisible thread. They became so plentiful and horrible that I pulled out the old mosquito net hat for the first time since Oregon. I crossed a few dirt roads, one of which led me to a fine broad trail distinctly marked PCT. It had a certain just-built freshness that should have warned me. Also, one set of footprints went one direction and back, and that should have warned me too; but I kept on it.

It made incredibly lazy switchbacks so that I was making very little uphill progress. But a splashing spring and the disappearance of all light put an end to the day. The steepness of the ridge forced a night on the trail, which wasn't bad at all. After a pot of rice and tomato soup mixed, I went to sleep.

September 2

I got a quick start, traversing the ridge as the sun began to melt away dark blue to light. The trail gave ominous telltale signs — a branch here, a bush on the trail there, and sure enough, the warnings were true; the trail stopped.

But the way was flagged, and underbrush was light, so I pushed on, following the flags. The most difficult part was walking on the slope; my ankles ached from turning constantly in one direction. I rounded the ridge and began another nightmarish fight through a grove of manzanita bushes. The grove became more and more impossible, until I came upon a deep gully lined with rocks. I could hear water far below.

With that I yelled a little and began to backtrack — the most frustrating of all experiences for a backpacker, just to know good and well that you're not going anywhere. Well, for the first time I knew there was no trail to follow, or at least knew it wasn't near me, and so began the map searching during lunch to plan a new way through this mess. Never again would I follow a new trail unless I saw it on a map.

Lunch was very meager — a banana and some bread and peanut butter. I had gotten just barely enough for three days, since I couldn't use my MasterCharge, and now I was looking at a tiny food supply — hardly enough for three days.

I struck up. Up always seems the best way to go when you're lost, and besides, I could follow an overgrown dirt road. Sure enough, I came upon a deer trail with an old temporary PCT marker, and I got to the ridgetop. Below I could still see but not hear I-5. Under a blazing sun I began down an old jeep trail, reaching a somewhat used dirt road.

No water since this morning, and I felt that old familiar dry, sandpapery giddy feeling of a great desire for water.

The dirt road turned to another jeep road, which ended on a ridge top. No trail. Nothing.

I followed deer trails, figuring animals knew best where water was, but the underbrush obscured them too. Down, down, down to the valley. I eventually began following a stream bed. Every third step my feet would slip on the steep incline covered with slick pine needles, and I'd come booming down on my rear and my sleeping bag. The descent became more and more difficult, until I finally yelled to all the outdoors: sky, trees, ground, everything, "I've had enough!" This was my theme song for a dirty, scraped crash to the valley bottom. Ahead was that glorious sight of a level, clear, smooth brown line — a road.

I rested by the dirt road for a while and walked down it to a stream. How convenient! Some wooden stairs took me to the stream, and I gulped a few good cups before setting up camp. I had really had enough. This bushwacking was wearing me thin. Camp was nestled in some grass at a bend in the road, where I had a good fire with some noodles for dinner.

> *How vain it is to sit down to write when*
> *you have not stood up to live!*
>> Henry David Thoreau
>> **The Journal of Henry D. Thoreau**

September 3

There is a time when one has to realize he has had enough. It isn't easy to say, but when finally admitted, it feels as if one has gotten to know oneself better. Then there can be as much pride in saying "I can't" as in "I can."

I thought hard about continuing on in this section. Now was my chance to experience the adventure that I had read about and dreamed the hike would be. This could be the stuff articles were written about. But as I looked at hardly a day's supply of food, after a breakfast which still left a hollow pit in my stomach, and knew that I had no reason to believe the trail ahead was any easier (hikers before me put a big question mark on these map sections as a guide), and so could very well have four days ahead of me, I decided to hike off the "trail." That decision was a relief, but it also left a hard pea of regret under a thousand mattresses of common sense. So I wouldn't have great stories[27] to tell my grandchildren. Even then, I also had some excitement about being a big step ahead so quick. It's such a breath of fresh air to be in a new segment.

So I began to follow a logging road out and away from the trail, down to lower elevations. Soon I came to the inevitable paved road, and after a couple of tries I was whisked away to a small town called McCloud. I couldn't believe it; the two guys who gave me a ride were trail builders. "Yeah, just skip this section; there's nothing here and the trail's not even finished." They told me about a trail builder who was killed in north Washington while working on some trail I had traveled.

Well, they dropped me off, and I went trudging up the highway occupied at my most despised pastime, hitchhiking. Huge logging trucks roared by, and after about thirty minutes of walking, I came to a couple of middle aged men who were talking about the ridiculous logging trucks which traveled back and forth going seemingly nowhere.

I saw they had a huge Americruiser, so I decided to give them a heartbreaking story so I wouldn't have to hitch any longer. I said I ran out of food, had to drop out, and could they give me a ride down to the highway? They said sure, and a large, kind lady stepped off the van and gave me a ham sandwich. The Mumbys then gave me a royal treatment to Burney Falls. Mrs. Mumby supplied me with a bowl of blackberries and whipped cream and washed out my water bottle while they let me shower. Last shower was in Seiad, I think. Mr. Mumby had said before we started, "Tom, it's not that I don't trust you, but ..."; and then he quietly walked to the back and pulled out a revolver and put it up front. "I just want to be safe." It hit me a little hard to think someone would worry that I might use their gun, but they had no reason to think otherwise, I guess. They were from near the Mexican border and told me how beautiful it was down there. I believe it.

As they dropped me off, Mr. Mumby said, "And if you ever write a book, I won't tell anyone you skipped part,"[28] and then he gave a big laugh. They were a wonderful group; I won't ever forget them.

I could now see Lassen Peak, a purple mountain with a little snow, all in the shape of an eagle's outspread wings. An old couple in a pick-up gave me a ride on into Burney. A trip to the P.O., bank, and to a sporting goods store for a plastic tarp to be used as a tent put me in a good stead for a while. I gorged myself on potato salad, tomatoes, milk, and doughnuts, and found an illegal place to sleep in someone's yard by a tree.

September 4

The night traffic kept me from a sound sleep; I thought that every approaching car would bring someone coming to tell me to leave.

For reason not recalled, Tom left the entry for September 4 incomplete. He departed Burney Falls on foot that day, followed the west rim of Hat Creek valley, and continued approximately twenty miles until meeting Highway 89 in the vicinity of Bridge Campground. Here he accepted a ride to Subway Cave, about five miles distant. He briefly visited the cave, then walked south about a mile to a point where he crossed Hat Creek on the slippery log.

I camped that night at a public campground. After a frantic, arm-waving traverse over a slippery log, I got some dry wood for a fire and had noodles for dinner.

Then I met two motorcycle couples about in their thirties; the '60s radicals turned into '80s conservatives going for a vacation fling on their motorcycles. After talking I went back to my sleeping bag, and one guy walked up to me. We looked at stars and talked of journeys. This was a personal, bond-forming conversation. So many people seem this way when I talk to them; they tell me of things they've done, bike trips or travels or hikes, as if those things are gone from their lives. They're almost pleading, trying to draw from me that feeling again, as if to say, I'm all right, aren't I? Even though now I live a sedate life, didn't I at one time really live and accomplish something? He became very quiet, and we said goodnight.

September 5

A crisp, breath-robbing cold morning. Indeed, the weather was getting chilly. I pushed on down the highway to the dirt road that would take me to the trail. I was so close now to the High Sierra — that last segment before my homestretch to the border, and the threat of the severe and unpredictable Sierra snowstorms.

But now the trail kept on a jeep road, where I passed a couple of great horned cows.[29] The land is so dry here — just sparse lodgepole pines with a fine carpet of needles, or a low, thick, tangled sea of bright green manzanitas. The trail cut a deep swath through these bushes, and I walked between two walls of green.

The landscape was lonely and a little eerie — all low, flat hills of the Modoc Plateau, which were perfectly symmetrical cones having been formed by layers of lava flow. All of these hills were carpeted with dark and light green, and presiding above all was purple Mt. Lassen, the wedge-shaped mountain with a cleft of snow on top.

The hiking was flat and easy as I entered Lassen Volcanic National Park. Again, I came upon a register box, where I could pick out several names of northbounders I had met long ago.

Very alone, I meandered through this flat land. After a lunch shared with ants and bees, I strolled by very flat, shallow, green lakes. I had taken a wrong turn, having planned on visiting the painted dunes and the Cinder Cone, an off trail attraction, but I eventually met the trail again. One couple set up their tent as I passed. Their time out here is so short, I hesitate to speak, and quietly walk by.

After weaving through mosquitoey marshland, I discovered a great campsite, a sandy area next to a large stream. Plenty of water! A filling dinner put me into a quiet, drifting sleep which melted away from a dazzling star display.

September 6

(I forgot about the Subway Cave, on September 5; it was flat floored, very chilly, very dark.) After breakfast I began up a slight forested incline to come to the edge of a cliff, the end of Flat Iron Ridge.

After passing a sign which warned of infected water and dangerous chipmunks, I continued along a valley where a group of people lolled in a man-made hot spring pool. They were far away, and I gazed on the little pink bodies, with their towels and flip flops,[30] imagining them all busily chattering away. My tug to get up the next hill matched the tug to go see them, so I followed a marked nature trail crossed by a warm, red stream.

Boiling Springs Lake hissed and rumbled, inviting a closer look, so I walked to the other side, watching the stream rise from the moving light-green water, which was surrounded by cracked, hissing potholes of clay. I had visions of what Bumpass Hell looked like, but the detour was too big to take.

After talking to a man with red hair and beard, and with a girl who told me to say hello to someone in Yosemite whom I think she called Bruce, I pounded on. A field of crunching, crackling yellow skunk cabbage brought me to the Terminal

Geyser, a jet engine of sorts jammed in the ground. I left my pack to check out this roaring fountain of steam, then reclaimed it and continued on.

I figured a dirt road would be shorter than the marked trail, and after a meager watered lunch, I moved on. While I sat next to the trickling stream source, a large branch broke off a tree across the road twenty feet away and crashed to the ground.

But a steamy, pounding hot sun made the day tiresome. I've been following some footprints which I think are Peter Wirth's. He seems to be sticking to the trail and so far has led me on some good decisions. (That hot pool with the group of people in it was Drakesbad.)

I gave directions to a passing couple of hunters, spoke with a lady who said she would have taken me in but her husband was in the hospital, and talked with a man who got out of his truck to tell me about the condition of some of the trail ahead.

After a wonderful drink and fill-up at Domingo Spring, I got lost for a few minutes and then crossed the Feather River on a huge steel bridge. Painful feet and my biweekly blister forced a stop at sunset. I get so frustrated when I have to stop like this, but a moderately good noodle dinner covered up my anger with a warm, heavy lump in my stomach. With no stream nearby, the silence was overwhelming.

September 7

The morning was crisp, cool, and clear, and I struck off in shorts and long-sleeved shirt, rounding knobs and manzanita bushes, clipping my fingernails and stroking my moustache while deep in thought. I was beginning to have to work at coming up with subjects to think about.

Among a net of dirt roads was Stover Camp, its existence

justified only by a cool marshy spring. I wove past some trailer campers fresh off a road, lying in lawn chairs and going to an awful lot of trouble to fix an elaborate breakfast with all the trimmings. They reported having seen a cougar fighting one of their dogs last night. The dog was tied to a trailer and giving a few yips at me as I passed by.

After a slightly confusing search, I bumped on downhill, and the familiar burning pit in the stomach forced a lunch stop just past a paved, busy road. Again it was weird to glimpse down the road as I crossed, watching the receding end of a trailer. A little peek back into a world that is now so alien to me.

(Idyllic view from the ridge here, a ribbon of a stream weaving across a flat, lush meadow with dark green trees dotting the landscape.) I enjoyed a quart of Kool-Aid with lunch and pushed on through flat land across Soldier Meadows and swampy Soldier Creek. Cattle gazed at me as I crossed the brackish but clear creek on a bridge and began the long climb up Butt Mountain.

The trail was built to be so slightly inclined that again I gained little altitude with miles of hiking, but it was pleasant. At a rest stop, I noticed that I was getting over the bout with diarrhea that I had been waging for a while.

I set my mind for the long climb and was lost in thoughts of backpacking at Davidson, supplied with fruit and doughnuts, when I noticed the sky was getting dark.

I covered my pack and placed my rain gear in my straps ready for rain. As I approached the ridge top among manzanitas, the storm began. Rain pelted around, some drops hitting my hood with a loud whap, and then a drenching downpour came, sticking my rainjacket to my skin. But the thunder was wonderful. I was near the very top of the ridge at 7,600 feet and so was in the choice balcony seat to hear the thunder in the valley below.

A large lake was still in sunshine in the distance, and the thunder exploded around me and then rolled and tumbled for several minutes back and forth through the valleys, slowly diminishing in volume. The lightening was at eye level, and the flashes sent a tingle through my back. I stood by a tree when the lightning left and watched the storm subside.

The show was wonderful, but wind picked up and I began to long for a warm camp. I passed up some windy ridgetop sites and surprised myself by hiking on until dark, when I set up my tarp across the trail between two trees and had a noodle dinner with some tantalizing bacon grease from Seiad Valley. I hoped some careless deer wouldn't run over me while trotting down the trail. For some reason I began to think of wolves, which frightened me, so I dozed off quickly.

September 8

Belden is nearby, and good reports from past hikers make me look forward to arriving there. With dreams of future hiking trips with Gia and Liza and John, I moved on down the ridge, taking a break for a while to look for water off the trail at a pass.

With full water bottles I moved on a level, weaving, exposed trail. The sky was clean from the previous day's rains, and the sharp winds that had herded the storm away still whipped around, making the hiking cool. After a steep segment, I stopped for lunch under a huge pine at Humboldt Summit. After lunch I found that two hikers had been near me behind a tree the whole time, their voices having been obscured by the wind. They had hiked from Welden through the High Sierra and were about to finish. We swapped water information, which was bleak for both parties, and after a talk went our separate ways.

I had on wool shirt and shorts, as the shade made the air quite cool, but the hiking was uneventful, so I contemplated C.S. Lewis while rubbing my moustache for a few miles, until I came upon a shallow spring near shimmering aspens. I almost mistook the sighing of the leaves for a large stream. I love those active trees; they stand alone among all the others as always being a welcome sight.

I camped that evening near a dirt road and, after heaving a charred stop sign out of the way, made a delightful fire with plenty of wood as dark closed in.

September 9

Today I reach Belden! These days always provide for quick awakenings and fast breakfasts. After a big granola meal I pushed on, making good tracks. At the top of a steep ridge I could look back and see the entire Lassen panorama on the horizon, with Lassen Peak wedged up amid the Cinder Cone and other volcanic hills. The distance made them blend with the ground in a dark blue-green. Some well-made signs gave rotten directions to Poison Spring, where I brushed my teeth and had a drink.

The trail became very haphazard, and I began to reminisce of the days up north as I began to again awaken some trail finding instincts. It's frustrating but very exciting to hike without a trail, and a nearby dirt road kept me on track.

From there on my guess was as good as the guidebook's, and I dropped into the headwaters of Chip's Creek canyon. A golden grassed meadow greeted me. What a rush of memories of Thanksgiving! Few portions of the hike did I enjoy as much as wandering down that meadow to lower altitudes where the air was cool, fall colors began to show, and an occasional swath of dead leaves crunched underfoot.

> *We are made to love the river and the*
> *meadow, as the wind to ripple the water.*
> Henry David Thoreau
> **The Journal of Henry D. Thoreau**

The creek was absolutely delightful, and I stocked up on water as the trail turned away, changing the crashing, frothing creek to a distant, unseen roar. The trail dropped endlessly on after a lunch stop in a moist meadow, from 5,000 to 2,400 feet. Little gnats began hanging before my eyes, and an approaching storm made for an exciting last few miles to Belden, miles which flew quickly by.

What a place! As I looked below, a tiny building made of logs sat nestled among some trees as a road, a river, and a toy-like train ran next to each other, winding together at the bottom of this steep canyon. As the cloud cover thickened, this little spot became more and more homey and inviting. After a twisting stomp down to the canyon floor and a quick stride across a small hydroelectric dam and the road, I entered Belden.

Several dogs ran by barking, and I came upon one of the few buildings, a wooden store and bar with pool table all in one. A few minutes later I was digging through a box of food, eating what I could there and inspecting a new camera, hammock, and other things (and a flashlight).

I called and wrote home as darkness began to fall with no rain. The owner of the store had a beautiful little blonde daughter, although he looked no older than me. As he worked, she would take off her shoes and walk barefoot on the pool table, having a blast.

A few workers strolled in bit by bit, and their conversation became more dulled as their beers sank into their minds. They would turn and eye me for a while and then join in a few more jokes. I wrote three letters while being in that little store for about four hours. It was so nice to sit inside at a table that I took my time, enjoying my anonymity and watching the workers move over to the pool table and the little girl getting sent off to bed.

The night was chilly, and I wavered down a back road until

I found a closed campground. Almost crawling because of the dark, I found a spot, ate a few cookies purchased at the store, scratched my feet, and fell asleep under a starless, inky black sky.

September 10

Under a gray cloud ceiling I took inventory of my feet. The moleskin seems to be causing the recurrent blisters on my heels, so I took it all off except for one patch and also took off some around my ankles which had been there almost three months.

The trail up was quite a change of pace as it zigzagged straight up the five thousand-foot slopes of Chip's Creek canyon. Views popped up every hundred feet or so, and Belden sank into the canyon depths until completely unseen, only the distant sound of a chain saw telling of its presence.

The little gnats also greeted me again; there seemed to be a nest on one side of the slope, and whining flies would cluster around me until I turned to the east slope, when they'd disappear.

I counted 116 switchbacks until reaching close to the top, where a chillly rain swept over the slope. I donned my rain gear and sat eating a package of Fig Newtons Momma had packed in my food box. The rain left, but bushes gilded with chilled water sopped my pants and boots.

At the top I could again see Lassen Peak behind me but could also see new canyons slicing through the peaks around me. All the mountains were green, but I could see granite knobs poking out at places — the sign that I had begun to hike the Sierra Nevada. I remember when back in Oregon I had dreamed so reverently of attaining that peak, and now I was past it.

The trail cut through higher and higher swaths of manzanita bushes, and tall weeds gave me a cold shower when I brushed them. Soon, though, the trail attained a gravelly base as I got to the top of the ridge. The clouds were low, and all the ridges around seemed to be exactly the same height, right at eye level. A stiff wind began to drive the clouds.

I skirted the ridge until stopping for lunch well before my planned destination, but an easy trail carried me on past Three Lakes and up Clear Creek, which seemed a little cow-infested to me. The sun began to break through as I left Clear Creek and headed towards Mt. Pleasant. I was surprised to already be there, and the sun became warm, so I shed on down to T-shirt and shorts.

The trail traversed a beautiful meadow, and I stopped to use my new camera for the first time. To my left the trail careened precipitously down past solid granite cliffs to a couple of dark blue lakes, cradled in the granite lap of one cliff.

That last little moleskin piece pulled up another blister, so I swore off moleskin forever and began to look for a campsite. I walked past Gold and Silver lakes until reaching a bend in the trail where I could camp in a clear grove near the ridgetop. A fogged breath told me the days were indeed getting colder; it seemed as if I was going to be racing the weather through the Sierra.

After pricking the blister and letting it empty, I had dinner, which was completed when I munched my entire supply of s'mores. The night chill grew deeper, and by a pleasant, warm fire I fell asleep.

September 11

The trail made a gentle descent on down through cow pasture meadows, and I passed a few wary herds. For the first time I accidently left my metal cup stuck in the bark of tree, where I usually put it while taking a break. I never want to lose that friend, so I backtracked and picked it up.

I switchbacked down through manzanita bushes and heard the crack of distant gunfire; deer season was still around and indeed I met a deer hunter coming up the trail with a bow and arrows in a quiver slung on his back. We talked for a while, but seeing that bow was a little frightening; I hope no one mistakes me for a deer.

I worked my way on down, in my mind telling people good choices to make in selecting equipment for a hike, realizing that I'm still a long way from having all the answers.

The trail stopped at a road at Bucks Summit, where I spent several minutes figuring out what was going on. Apparently a new trail had been built, which meant my guidebook wouldn't be a big help for a while. I studied the map posted by the road, and then plunged into another grove of manzanitas to start up another slope.

The altitude was only about six thousand feet, so the heat began to build up, and soon I was working up the ridge in shorts and T-shirt. A wonderful cool stream invited me to stay for lunch on a soft mat of pine straw in cool shade. I had deviled ham sent from home, a real treat. A lengthy reading of *Mere Christianity* made me antsy to move on; so back on with the damp inner socks, the outer wool socks, and the boots.

There seemed to be many more streams than the map indicated, so I knew I couldn't trust it very much from here on. A beautiful meadow floated by, the kind one dreams of camping in, with deep shady limb cover and dark green grass; but I had to move on.

I passed two guys putting up a large PCT sign by Road 24N29Y. I was on the right track. After switchbacking up another hill, to my left loomed an unimpressive view of small, dirt road-crossed hills. Back down again. But again I left my cup hanging on a wooden sign telling the bleak story of little water ahead, and I had to backtrack again. Am I losing my head? Twice in one day, yet never before!

As I retraced my steps this time, bushes below me on the steep ridge began to shake, and I could hear some loud gruffing. It stopped as soon as I passed, so I whistled along, trying to make noise in case it was another bear. No problem, but I was always on the lookout as I descended deeper and deeper into the canyon of the Middle Fork of the Feather River.

As the shadow of the ridge crept up the opposite canyon slope, I continued on down, and the distant roar of the river began to emerge. Spurred on by plenty of water, I moved on down a seemingly endless trail as night began to darken. The effects of lower altitude were apparent: a little more close, or humid; more hardwoods; and the little gnats hanging in front of my face.

The river never showed itself that evening, and I camped thankfully by a crashing, cool tributary. Tonight I tried a new dish of mashed potatoes with gravy. What a discovery! The potatoes became a little thin, but there was plenty, one-third of the box of instant, and they left a good solid block in my stomach. I hung my food, a very clumsy attempt at best, for the sound of the bear above still kept me a little uneasy.

No bears bothered me, but a family of ants did. Apparently due to a poor choice of campsite, I spent all night mashing black ants as they would trickle over my face, across my legs, or up and down my side. I remember being partially asleep and still picking those things off me. I didn't get much rest this night.

September 12

Eager to see the Feather River, I hurried on down in the chilly canyon before the sun had a chance to warm things up. After washing dishes and taking pictures of what I thought was the Feather River, I hiked up to a saddle. How could this be? I was about five miles farther back than I thought. Night comes more quickly in a canyon, and apparently I went to sleep too early last night.

At the real Feather River, a huge hiker's bridge spanned across it thirty feet in the air. Clustered at the river side were sandy shores and milky white rocks sculpted smooth by the constantly swirling water.

I took another break and sat on a boulder, taking pictures. The pressure of moving on always makes me try to sort out exactly where I want to stop and spend some time seeing a beautiful place, so up on the bridge I took another rest. The knowledge of being three miles behind, plus having stopped at two rivers, one of which I erroneously thought was the Feather, made me languid and depressed. This rock-jewelled river was so cool and restful, I wanted so much to stay, and the knowledge of today's long uphill and of the hundreds of uphills to come fell like a weight. God, I didn't want to move.

> *Let me not live as if time was short.*
> *Catch the pace of the seasons; have*
> *leisure to attend to every phenomenon of*
> *nature, and to entertain every thought*
> *that comes to you.*
>
> Henry David Thoreau
> **The Journal of Henry D. Thoreau**

Onion Valley was below me, but I made the mistake of waiting to get water higher up. Up and away from the gnats I climbed, thinking of my brothers and sisters at home. I kept coming to gullies in the ridge, but no tinkling sound of water was in them. Dogwood Creek, a hopeful source, was dry. The guidebook promised a lake, but the trail wound around so much I couldn't begin to find it; and its outlet was dry. At the ridgetop I met a confluence of jeep roads and hunted down these for a while, still with no luck. Upset, I bounded across dry stream beds yelling, "California is the WORST state in the country!" After whining awhile I pushed on up, dry and lunchless, as the afternoon began to wear on. A half mile down, another dirt road finally led me to a deep cool spring embedded in a meadow below the trail. Two trips to it washed down my lunch and stocked me up for dinner.

I could only hike a few more miles before darkness began to fall, so I camped at a saddle on the ridge, in an open spot near a thick forest. A trail post and a tree served as tying posts as I tried for the first time to build a decent tent out of my tarp. The wind was fairly cold, but I thought it wise to practice anyway. It was cramped, but it did the job.

September 13

A very chilly morning, and I got going in shorts and wool shirt, rubbing my hands together. Soon my tight and cramped legs got moving, and I made good time over some tricky trail, referring to my guidebook many times. From the north a wind was coming, and a few miles away was a foreboding bank of black clouds.

Soon I came to a dirt road where a logger was standing, bundled up in coat, gloves, and hat. I felt a little out of place, but I left my pack to drop down the road a ways to utilize a sure water source. Back at the top we talked a little, and he described the joys of making as much money as he was and said it might snow today.

I wouldn't believe him. I didn't feel it was that cold. After some confusing wandering, I went back down the same road and saw the familiar little metal diamond nailed to a tree. Walking up a slope, through dry skunk cabbage crackling underfoot, I crossed a meadow, passing a tall snow depth gauge. After much guidebook consultation, I found the trail and rounded Pilot Peak.

The wind continued to pick up. I wove in and out of hills,

moving along the ridge top. As I came out of the forest to an exposed hill, it broke. The black clouds had reached my ridge, and a freezing wind whipped over the top. My hands, face, and legs went numb, and then sleet and hail began to patter around me.

I virtually ran over the next bare hills until I found a spot with trees and, under my tarp, donned every piece of clothing I had in my pack. The hail made a loud but pleasant pattering, and feeling dry and warm, I ate lunch and read some C.S. Lewis while sitting by my pack under the tarp on a big tree root.

The change was incredible. I had on mittens, hat, everything, whereas minutes before I had been hiking in my shorts. I can see how some people can freeze by failing to plan for bad weather.

I hiked on, the cloud cover dropping the temperature drastically. The trail was new and evident, though, so time passed quickly.

At Nelson Creek I took a water break and started up another canyon. This cold wintery weather makes me think of home so much, I hike almost with eyes closed and dream. I goaded myself past some beautiful campsites on up to the top of the canyon where it seemed all the wind collected. A violent wind whipped branches, me, pack, bushes, everything. I wanted to take a picture of the boiling black sky, but standing still enough was difficult. Only after crunching down on my knees could I do it.

The wind died slightly as I rounded Gibralter Rock, but so did something else — the trail. With no visual obstructions, however, I had little trouble following some flags. The only problem was wading through the manzanitas. Soon, though, the flags died too, and the clouds dropped around me to form a fog with a rain shower.

That was enough for me, so I wedged myself in between two

trees and made dinner, after trying several times to get the stove started. That dull, soft roar came burping out though, and I had a hot dinner.

The weather scares me. I really don't know if I'll be able to finish the trail. Already I'm getting heavy storms, and in a month I'll be in the High Sierra, with trail elevations up to twelve thousand feet. I'm cutting it close, that's for sure. I wrapped up in the tarp as in a cocoon and said goodbye to the storm.

September 14

My guidebook has written in it, "follow flags," but no flags are to be seen. After a quick breakfast, the sky was scoured clear by a strong wind, and I began looking for a trail, sadly anticipating another fight through the bushes. I kept following what I thought were deer trails; but deer can go under branches people can't, and so inevitably I was pushing through branches. A thick forest was closing in.

I kept a good, steady altitude, and in the distance I saw a blue ribbon tied to a tree, fluttering in the breeze. What a beautiful sight. It was like a friend, flashing between the trees trying to catch my attention. When I reached that one, I could find another on through the trees waving to me. My pace quickened as I went down a series of switchbacks.

Then the trees opened to show a wide sea of manzanita bushes, and my stride came to a dead stop. The little ribbons were fluttering across an impossible ocean of tangled, springy, sharp branches. I tried to detour them, but the slope became too steep below, and I resigned myself to a bushwack.

For three hours (I guess) I didn't touch ground. The bushes were so thick I had to walk on them, and it seemed as if every twig was reaching out and grabbing me or my pack. At times I was flipped upside down and became a yelling, cursing maniac.

I prayed to be transported out of this mess. The bushes kept going on and on and on.

I took a break at a slight clearing. In the distance far below lay a smooth brown ribbon, a dirt road. That kept me going on. The road, however, was not on the map, but I decided to take my chances. To the point of desperation, I crashed downhill. After a while — sweating, bleeding, and hot — I swung out on a tree branch and dropped to the road.

What a joy to walk on hard ground without interference! It's funny how I can complain about hiking until having to bushwack, and then have trail hiking seem like heaven. A small stream splashed across the road a few yards ahead. After refreshing myself and resting, I moved on; and the road did come out where it should have, and I was finally back on the trail. I met a motorcycle rider who was all bundled up. I expressed my fears of approaching winter to him, and he said the heavy snows won't come until October. Great.

The dirt road became a wide trail, and eagerness to get to Sierra City pushed me on. After lunch atop a chilly wind-swept ridgetop, clouds began to swirl in again. I met a tall bearded man walking with a short English girl and talked with them awhile. They were hiking the state of California; he's had to resole his shoes twice!

It was a pleasant conversation, but we all pushed on. They recommended Packer Lake Lodge, so I set my sights on it and picked up the pace. I got lost for a minute at Deer Lake but found my way on. Surrounded by cliffs, with my way lit by a brightening dusk moon, I had to urge myself on past there. A beautiful lake, so quiet. The streams I crossed were difficult, but after lots of arm waving and big leaps, I got across each of them. The trail kept on crossing down a rocky ridge, and darkness kept falling. My dreams of Packer Lake Lodge put me into a run. For three miles I ran over streams and down the trail, until I couldn't see clearly anymore. But a road appeared, a paved one. Following

"Um, can I have some dinner?"

it under the light of the moon, I rounded Packer Lake until I came to the soft yellow lights of cabins. A phone rang, which made me jump. I was very nervous, but I set my pack on the porch and opened the door. I had no idea how cold it was outside until I walked into the dining area. A warm fire blazed on the left, and a few people at tables talked and laughed. So warm.

My boots make me feel clunky and awkward when indoors; I felt conspicuous. An older woman in a red windbreaker asked if she could help me, and I asked if I could get dinner here. Why do I feel so stupid? My insides are tight. The waitress popped out, arms laden with plates, and without realizing it I was standing in her way. "Um, can I have some dinner?" I asked sheepishly. "Okay! okay! Just let me serve these people!" she said exasperatedly. I sat down. God, I've lost all ability to talk to people it seems. I almost left. After a big cheeseburger and ice cream, I felt better. Classical guitar on an unseen stereo and the crackling fire made me nearly weep; it reminded me of home so much.

Soon I was by the fire writing home and talking to a few people. The lodge owner, a thin, very old-looking man dressed in contemporary disco-type clothes, offered me the porch to sleep on. He made fun of my southeastern accent and my calling him sir. It was wonderful to be talking to people who had nothing to do with a trail or backpacking.

The frigid night air was intensified after my stay indoors. Some guy (I think he was drunk) told me he was from the FBI and talked with me for about a minute; and soon, after all were in bed, I spread my sleeping bag on the flat porch and slid in. Such a change this evening was.

September 15

I got up when the sun cracked the frigid air with a warm light and walked the short distance back to the trail as a lone, early-rising fisherman sat in his boat in the middle of Packer Lake. With thoughts of returning home, I climbed up to the last ridge, which stood like a wall between me and Sierra City. Boy, what a reunion that will be. I hope they give me a flight home.

At the ridgetop, I received a beautiful sight of Sierra Buttes. After a few pictures I started down, walking above the Sardine lakes among bushes. After a private discourse on what makes a person happy, I came to the last dirt road, which soon came to a paved road; and after being windswept by a couple of logging trucks, I came to a major road.

At the wrong place, however. I was about five miles further east of Sierra City than I should have been. A clear blue sky above sharply contrasted green mountains was displayed before me as I walked on down. Now this is what I thought the Sierra would be like.

Soon a friendly old man gave me a ride to the town, about four miles away. It was a very quaint, quiet, one-street town, and without hesitation I stepped into the P.O. and was soon reading letters and eating ham and cheese straws. Past notes of hikers (including one from long lost Peter Wirth) warned northbounders of the ratty condition of the trail they had ahead of them.

While at the little store I met two southbounders, one from Roswell, Atlanta! They were hiking a section, and we became friends fast. After munching out together on bananas and milk and doughnuts, we took some pictures of each other.

My call home was a joy as usual, but my parents' as well as my own fears of entering the High Sierra were obvious. I would try to make it seem not so bad, and Dad said, "Now, son, you have to admit you haven't been completely honest with us." I had to agree. The High Sierra are still two weeks away, and the past recent storms make me quite apprehensive. I decided to go ahead and hitch the next forty miles of trail, since it was all roads anyway and time was getting precious. That would save two days.

The two hikers offered a camping spot, but I told them my predicament and decided to move on. I didn't look forward to this. I *hate* hitchhiking; to depend on someone else to travel. I feel like such a leech.

A couple gave me a ride a few (eight) miles, and then I was plunked on a flat road. I was wholeheartedly depressed. Out of my element and away from a trail, I slogged down the road past lonely, vast cow pastures pitted with tree stumps. The mountains were to my right and, as the sun dropped, I uneasily contemplated camping on someone's property. What a lost feeling. No longer a hiker but a wayfarer. I took a masochistic joy in counting how many more cars went the opposite direction than ones that would take me where I wanted to go.

Then an old Plymouth pulled over, and a man with a stray eye offered a ride. He was fascinated by the hike, and soon we talked of his climbs on Mt. Shasta and my time on the trail. He gave me a ride to Truckee and then all the way to Donner Pass and back to the trail![31] His name is Ralph Thomas, and he lives part-time in Dalton, Georgia!

At Norden, a little town near the trail, he bought several candy bars for me, all the while telling this cute girl behind the counter of my hike. She smiled but wasn't at all impressed, and then he offered to give me a place to stay at the Sierra Grub Hut. What a wonderful guy. He truly gave of his time and money, and he sparked me for the high mountains coming up. I'll never forget him.

That night I showered at the hut and read a little C.S. Lewis in the small reading room. Sitting in that wooden bunk room and staring through an open window at an inky black sky pulled out a lot of emotions. The cold air reminded me of my favorite season at home, and I really wondered whether I wanted to go through this next month. I was getting scared thinking of being at over twice the altitude I had been so far, with the weather the coldest it's ever been.

September 16

A fabulous breakfast! With about ten guests at the hut, I ate fruit and yogurt, sausage and eggs, and pancakes and cereal. Across from me sat an old, baldheaded and white-bearded man who seemed at the peak of health and had a Swedish accent. He talked of his times in the High Sierra and urged me to continue. While clearing up, someone began whistling Bach, and we all joined in washing pots, pans, and dishes. Soon they had all gone their separate ways — hiking, reading, or whatever; and with a bag lunch I started out at 9:00 A.M. Thank you, Ralph Thomas, for a wonderful time!

Under a blazing blue sky I walked past some construction and out of Norden, back towards the trail. The road went by several cabins near Ice Lakes, where people sitting on their lawns waved, and soon it gave way to dirt. Two rangers offered me a ride to the trailhead two miles away. I accepted, and after a bouncing, banging ride down, I changed into shorts and began a walk past several NO TRESPASSING signs. A man nearby told me a new trail had been built several thousand feet up a far ridge. That was my main goal for the day.

After passing the day hikers I hit the real trail and began a long trudge up the American River. The river provided companionship with its rushing and splashing, as well as a constant water supply, and the hike was pleasant. The ridges on either side were typically Sierra Nevada — a paucity of trees but beautiful green slopes of grass. I got lost once after taking a wrong turn, but felt that subconscious nagging that I wasn't where I should be, checked the maps, and was back on track after a couple of miles of searching.

The trail crossed a mushy, reedy section of the stream and then shot straight up the canyon side. After panting up that section, I met a huge sign that announced, NOW OPEN! THE PACIFIC CREST TRAIL! Where are the balloons and dancing girls and free champagne?

I kept pushing upwards as light began to recede, past a tempting campsite. The water seemed too impure, so I pushed on. In the half-light of dusk a buck and a doe passed fifty yards ahead of me, and for a few minutes I tried to capture them on film, but they didn't seem to want to have their picture taken.

On the eastern slope of Granite Chief, I made camp with a large, crackling fire. The water supply was deep in some moss, and I could get some only after pressing my cup into the moss and filling up my water bottle cup by cup. A dinner of Ramen concluded the day, and I went to sleep under a chilly black sky next to the quietly sighing embers of my fire.

September 17

I started the morning climbing up a steep wall surrounding a beautiful little meadow below, and at eight thousand feet I could see the Crystal Range, the first solid granite mountains I've seen yet. Lake Tahoe is down there somewhere. A pleasant trail wound among skunk cabbage and reeds past some good streams as another gray cloud cover began to slide over the sky. The owner of Packer Lake Lodge had said the winter storms had begun, while others had said that they hadn't, so I didn't know what to think.

A brand new soft trail led off to my left, but with visions of bushwacking fresh in my mind, I descended on a longer but surer trail to Five Lakes Creek.

The cloud cover and the easy grade of the valley floor made for pleasant hiking. At Bear Pen Creek I had lunch with some uninvited ants and, after a couple of hairy creek crossings, started up the Powderhorn Creek valley. A horse train passed, and as I continued up, I found a box of cookies one member had dropped. It had been trampled but not destroyed, and I gratefully packed it away.

Columnar andesitic lava flows hung above me on the canyon wall, like vast dirt dauber nests clinging to the ridge.

Thoughts of Margaret and Randy sifted through my mind, and after a good water stop among head-high bushes and reeds, I pushed on up. At the top of the pass was the road the horses had come from, and I moved down large dirt road switchbacks until joining the trail again at Barker Meadow.

I took a chance on some new trail, which led me over manzanita covered hillocks back to a dirt road. A few miles down these deeply rutted swaths of dirt I found a good halting spot after a few leaps across a stream.

The cloudy sky still threatened rain, and accordingly I laid out the tarp under a tree, ready to roll up in it. A huge fire cooked some Kraft Macaroni & Cheese (a good success), and cookies! and hot Jell-O. No rain that night, but just as I was about to doze off, a heavy, soft fuzzy thing landed on my stomach, apparently after having lept out of the tree. He ran away, knocking over my water bottles, before I could turn on the flashlight to see what he was.

> *Next day I returned to town and was disappointed as usual in obtaining money. So after spending the day looking at the plants in the gardens of the fine residences and town squares, I returned to my graveyard home. That I might not be observed and suspected of hiding, as if I had committed a crime, I always went home after dark, and one night, as I lay down in my moss nest, I felt some cold-blooded creature in it; whether a snake or simply a frog or toad I do not know, but instinctively, instead of drawing back my hand, I grasped the poor creature and threw it over the tops of the bushes. That was the only significant disturbance or fright that I got.*
>
> John Muir
> **A Thousand-Mile Walk to the Gulf**

September 18

The sky is still overcast, and a light rain periodically spatters around. I got lost once I had started and had to backtrack several times as the myriad of old logging roads crossed and recrossed the trail, obliterating it completely. Accompanied by the distant sound of chain saws and logging trucks roaring in the forest, I finally found myself by Miller Meadows. The marshy creek there offered little pure water, so I walked past an old dilapidated cabin and up a jeep road. The rain forced me to put on all my rain gear, even though it only came every other minute or so.

After splashing through water-soaked underbrush down to General Creek, I sat and enjoyed the last candy bar Ralph Thomas had given me. Climbing past the dry headwaters, the trail hit an easy grade. But spirits are low: the heavy cloud cover scares me a little and makes the air chilly, just enough to slightly numb my fingers. I ate lunch under a pleasant tree cover. Lord, I'm tired. My shoulders ached.

Sometimes I can't get going; I guess I'm just out of it mentally, and now I slogged past the Velma lakes, stopping every one-half mile or so to rest. I wanted to get over Dicks Pass before the day was out, and I could see the 9,300-foot high granite wall I had to climb to get over it. Heavy dark storm clouds continually slid through the pass.

At Fontanillis Lake I met a heavily bearded guy in a down coat trying with trouble to set up a tent in the rising wind. "The winds are about 50 mph at the pass, so be careful with your pack. Go for it." It was the last thing I wanted to do. I thanked him and began the wide arc up the ridge above Dicks Lake. The wind kept getting higher and higher.

The trail even climbed up above the pass, and soon I was cursing the trail and the weather. Wind would yank my pack and myself from side to side, and my feet and hands began to hurt. Man, how it screamed through a few timber pines that clung to the bare pass. For some reason I didn't think to put on my wool sweater and cap and mittens. The conditions gave me nightmarish daydreams of vomiting blood and dying in the Sierra Nevada. As I descended on the other side, I just kept yelling, "I want to go home!" It felt good to get that out. Below was Desolation

Valley, a nearly bare valley of tumbled granite, with lakes dotting the floor in every hole.

Towards this I descended, and my head began to clear a little. Looking back on it, I really think I had begun to get hypothermia at the pass. Few times have I desired a warm home so much.

At Gilmore Lake I passed a few camps, one of which had a Starflite tent just like the one I had lost so long ago. Without hesitation I just whipped up a huge pot of instant rice and split peas, then climbed in my sleeping bag and rolled up in my tarp. I also had a box of butter pecan pudding, and with this warm meal in my stomach, I began to warm up. The wind is still high, though, and keeps blowing my tarp off me. God, it's cold.

September 19

Today I began a three-day rest from the trail. I walked through Desolation Valley, through the maze of granite and streams and lakes, under a breezy and chilly blue sky. At Lake Aloha I had an early lunch, still in a nearly treeless land. A helicopter swooped down the valley, around the lake, and away again. After my prunes and peanut butter and honey, I pushed on, seeing more and more backpackers as I went. I was getting near my destination. I stopped and took a picture for a group of hikers. They said they thought the winter storms had begun. Great.

Past Tamarack Lake I met up with a white-bearded old man walking with a cane and accompanied by a little beagle that had its own pack. We talked for a good couple of miles; what a great guy. He had been in the mountains for the weekend, and he gave me a detailed map of Lake Tahoe, where I was headed. He also said that a casino had been bombed, so the all-you-can-eat restaurant wasn't there any longer. He was a Christian, and we talked and talked until he stopped to have a rest. I had to move on in order to get off the trail in time, and soon I rounded the Echo Lakes. I signed the register there and had some water; then I found two girls and a guy who said they would give me a ride down to Lake Tahoe. It was a pleasant drive, and after they stopped being uneasy, we talked more and more until they dropped me off at the "Y," a meeting place of three highways. They helped me orient myself there, and I said thank you many times.

First I dropped off my boots to have them resoled at a boot repair shop. Ready by Monday. Then to the bank to take out some more money. A teller said that it had snowed here a few weeks ago! Geez, I don't believe it! Soon I began my pilgrimage to the Nevada-California border to find one of those all-you-can-eat restaurants.

A girl (a nurse) gave me a ride, and soon I was plunged deep into the heart of the most purely human, man-made place I'd ever been. Lights flashed, screaming who was entertaining where; posters of dancing girls everywhere; lines of casinos with thousands of people behind glass windows yanking one-armed bandits; and so much traffic. We had a pleasant talk, though, and she let me off at the Sahara-Tahoe, a $2.00 all-you-can-eat!

I moved about in the sea of human bodies inside the casino until a manager saw me and said, "You, sir, cannot come in here with that pack." So I took it off outside, returned, and he escorted me right back out again. I think God doesn't want me to eat here. I went across the highway to a smaller casino and explained my predicament. That past bombing has everyone scared, and I can't carry my pack around anywhere. They agreed to hold my pack, and I sneaked back into the Sahara-Tahoe, to the end of a huge line. It took over an hour to get seated, during which time I watched people going crazy over the one-armed bandits and also found a $1.00 discount dinner ticket. Some people even left the line and skipped dinner to gamble, they'd get so excited. I read *Mere Christianity* some and met an older couple with their daughter. The four of us descended upon the buffet tables. I had arrived while there was still light in the

"You, sir cannot come in here with that pack."

sky, and I stayed until 11:30 p.m. I would eat and read and read and eat until I almost exploded. My stomach was so tight that I couldn't begin to bend over.

Back out into the chilly night air, I retrieved my pack and walked the couple of miles back to a campground I had seen before. My feet were in tennis shoes, since I had given up my boots, and the freedom they gave my feet made them ache. They're so unused to bending.

I refused to pay someone five dollars to sleep on a tiny patch of ground, after being able to sleep on most any ground I wanted to for the past four months, so I snuck under the fence and just rolled out my bag. I felt for sure I would get kicked out, for I felt a very sharp pain on my scalp, like something was gnawing on it; and later my eyes opened to a stabbing white light shining right in my eyes. I never figured out what either of those things were.

September 20

A very lazy day. I went to a grocery store and bought food for today and tomorrow, wrote letters, did laundry, looked in an art gallery, and walked on the beach until dinner time came around; then I decided to go back to the Saraha-Tahoe. A guy at a gas station agreed to hold my pack for me (I decided to take the chance), and I walked packless down to the place again.

This time I met a single middle-aged man who gave me another dollar discount ticket. We sat and munched prime rib, crab salad, scallops — a never-ending variety. He left, but I continued to eat and read a little. The waiter walked by and rapped his knuckles on my table. The waiter last night had kept on urging me to eat more, but this guy makes me uncomfortable. A huge, muscular guy with long blond hair past his shoulders sat down next to me with a beautiful girl. He asked what I was reading. I showed him the *Mere Christianity* book. "Read Jesus, man," he said. "He's the real thing."

After an hour or so more, I was so full that I felt almost sick. Eventually a man leaned over my shoulder. "I'm sorry, sir, but you'll just have to leave. Our waiter makes his money on this table." That made me feel terrible. I had to get out of this place, to just get away from people whose primary objective is obtaining money. I got up with difficulty and waddled to a restroom, where I sat digesting for almost thirty minutes. Then followed a long, chilly walk back to get my backpack and on back to the campsite. That night someone and his dog almost stepped on me, and the beam from another flashlight struck me in the eyes. The sky is clear tonight.

September 21

I'm going to try to go to church today! I filled up on Life cereal and washed up in a service station restroom. I feel like such a bum, living trail life in a civilized city; this is depressing. The group at the church were very cordial, and I met a couple of guys my age who had hiked parts of the California trail. The minister was from Haiti, very sincere and animated but not very impressive. I don't know, I guess I just don't think anything quite measures up to home life. I felt more and more grungy, seeing the clean, powdered, fresh-scented people around me, and was a little glad to leave. But still it was a refreshing experience. One girl sang during the service — a beautiful voice. I called Mom and Dad, Margaret and Randy, and Barbara and Kenny.[32] Barbara is on the verge of having another baby, and I was the first to hear of a false alarm last night. I received a lot of "be carefuls" and was very replenished, although a little sad after the calls.

I had lunch on the shore of Tahoe and for some reason talked myself out of taking a swim. I read some more, wrote letters, and finally finished *Mere Christianity*. What a great book.

When dinner time rolled around, I fixed up a pot of gummy noodles on the beach and just couldn't force it down. So I had a slow dinner in a nearby Sambo's, finishing with some hot chocolate. On the beach, a man wearing a suit had walked up behind me and asked what I was doing. I told him, and he said, "Well, that's great." Then he looked at me and said, "But you've been hitchhiking, haven't you?" Boy, I love it when people say that. Having hiked nearly the entire way to date, I am sensitive about such comments, and I told him about the hike.[33]

A chilly night fell, and again I walked a slow, uneasy walk back to the campground. Some guy with a guitar was hitching a ride. I talked with him for a second, but I realized that I was hurting his chances of getting someone to stop, so I moved on. One last night in the campground, and the owner will be free of me forever. The pine straw floor and few pine trees make me think so much of home; and the sky is beautiful, absolutely clear. It is my only reminder of the world in the mountains, as it is the only thing yet untouched by man here in Lake Tahoe.

> *It appears to be a law that you cannot*
> *have a deep sympathy with both man and*

nature. Those qualities which bring you
near the one estrange you from the other.
Henry David Thoreau
The Journal of Henry D. Thoreau

September 22

Out, out, out of here! After a good breakfast on the beach (I took some pictures for a black couple walking on the beach), I got ready to go. I emptied my pack and gave it a good cleaning. Stopped by the P.O. too.

A couple in a pickup quickly gave me a ride down the wild early morning highway, back to the "Y." My shoes were ready and looked like they had had a good resoling job. It was neat walking on new soles that seemed to grab the ground. I gave them a good water-proofing and then walked over to the grocery.

After packing up food enough for about two weeks and eating lunch, I was finally trying to hitch a ride back to the trail. The clear weather has been an anxiety; those clear days are ones I could've used to get through the Sierra. But my boots had to be resoled. Now I was eager to go and make tracks before something hit.

But no ride for a while. A pleasant man in a VW with a sweet dog gave me a ride for a short distance. Then as the sun began to cast long shadows, a station wagon with four people stopped — two guys and two girls. I climbed in, and we talked away as the car climbed back up the mountains to the ridgetops. One guy gave me a fake ticket or something so that I could have a free ride on a train. I never quite understood what he was talking about.

At Little Norway, by Lower Echo Lake, where I had stopped three days before, I finally met the trail again. I said goodbye to the group and had to backtrack a little until I found the trail.

It was nice to be back again, but I didn't feel like hiking. Eating real food for three days gave me a sickly sweet, nauseous feeling in my full stomach, and diarrhea hit again. I only made it a mile before it hit a second time. I had to bury some underwear, it was so bad. I seem to have absolutely no control over myself. My body determines what it's going to do, and I have no choice.

I lay on the trail without a fire and had some doughnuts for dinner. I've begun the section I wanted so much to begin. As I dozed off, an ant ran across my face. He seemed to be saying, "Welcome back!"

September 23

A beautiful day. Walking is easy. I finished off the doughnuts from Tahoe and got off to a good start. I lost the trail for a second near a lake in a half frozen, half marshy meadow. After crunching through that I passed a couple with an elaborate camp-site who were frying bacon.

The sun is strong, but my breath curls up in a wisp of fog, and I have on cap, mittens, and sweater. A steep shady climb made me warm up, and soon I began to peel off outer clothes.

Up to a plateau on an easy roller coaster of a trail I went, passing a large lady pounding by with her son, she declaring that the trail was very easy. I kept on climbing until I popped over a ridge. In the middle of a sloping meadow was a large patch of snow glistening in the sun. It's been July since I've seen that much snow, and it looked like a UFO that had just landed; it seemed so out of place. Near a tall, reedy, marshy slope I had a good lunch of peanut butter, honey, and nuts and then moved on. I have only one bag of nuts for this entire section (for lunch); I'll be cutting it close food-wise, for sure.

The trail is very gneissic; granite is everywhere. I can see Tahoe, or slight glimpses of it, below me.

Soon, though, I started up the Upper Truckee River canyon, past a few herds of cattle. The canyon is very wide, shallow, and filled with a huge green meadow. In the middle was a tiny flash of light, the metal roof of a cabin.

I was curious about it but moved on. The river is very wide and shallow, so I can walk across it without getting more than my soles wet. I knew I was nearing a road, for I began to see a few people. Weather still nags me, and I asked them about past conditions. Turns out it has already snowed once or twice.

Sure enough, I came to Highway 88 and became confused as to where the trail ran. After following an abandoned road, I came to it at Carson Pass. At the pass a crowd of guys and girls my age stood laughing hilariously at something. A statue stood there, just a big broken obelisk, possibly commemorating some early explorer. Oh well. The group drove off as I approached, so I just hiked right onto the trail, past a Forest Service Information Station which had a bulletin warning about the severity of winter storms.

Up a huge rock wall, and then I came to Frog Lake. Here the trail ended. While I sat pondering whether to strike off in trailless country, a beautiful red-haired woman in her thirties approached with a backpack. She was a professional photographer, and we talked of the beauty of this section. After seeing on the map the stuff she had been pounding through, I concluded that she was a very hardy lady. For some reason that was a very pleasant encounter, although a short one. She seemed to be a very intense person, one of the few I've ever met who looked at you when you or they were talking.

The sun was dipping low, so I began to make camp near rocky-shored Frog Lake. By the time I had a good roaring fire going, the moon had appeared, again full. One month ago I was walking in the Marble Mountains under a full moon; a month before that, in the middle of Oregon under a full moon. Before that, in the high snows of the Cascades. And yet I still have almost two more moons to go. The thought of that was so painful. I couldn't even begin to imagine what it would be like to be home.

September 24

The day began with a problem. There's no trail. But there is also little vegetation up here, and periodically a little ribbon under a rock marks the trail, so I struck out over the Elephant's Back. Round Top, a jagged row of black rock gutted with snow, lay to my right. After some map consultation, I walked through a deep snow patch (the crunch of snow brought back memories of June!) and eventually found the trail. The Nipple, an odd mountain true to its name, sat off to the distance. An unusual volcanic landscape.

While walking up new trail, I saw a little, skinny, bushy-tailed fox digging in his own (or something else's) den. First time I've seen one. I got a couple of pictures, but soon I came too close, and he took off.

The trail met a road at a saddle, where I decided to not trust the new section any longer, and I followed a temporary route past Upper Blue Lake and Lower Blue Lake. I passed a couple of bearish looking guys in a pickup; a Frenchman who was hiking to "Zee Nee-pool" (the Nipple); and, by the lakes, several car campers who were fishing. The water supply was plentiful, and at the stream between the two lakes, I had lunch on a picnic table. I'm now starting *Crime and Punishment*.[34]

The pleasant stream was difficult to leave, but in about a half an hour of hiking I had regained the real trail at an oversized parking lot off the dirt road. I began to leave the trailer campers behind as I weaved through granite outcrops, hillocks, and saddles. Near Summit Lake was a confluence of roads (five), so I deliberated for a while and then struck off down one to find a herd of cattle polluting a good water source. They panicked and began a wild earth-shaking sprint down the trail, except for one stupid cow and her calf who ran up, then began their careening descent down towards me. With a cloud of dust, they made a hairpin turn when they saw me and trundled on down the slope after their friends. This could get to be dangerous.

The sun began to hover low over the horizon, and the slope became steeper and steeper and more and more devoid of vegetation. The loose volcanic soil can't hold very much. This landscape is really bizarre. To my left the trail drops almost vertically down eight hundred feet, and mounds of volcanic outcroppings cling to the ridge side. The ridge is very convoluted, so I find myself walking in and out, in and out. A hopeful source was dry, but soon I found a campsite on this slope. An island of trees had established a hold on a flat outcrop, and here I camped, with some trouble in maintaining secure footing while trying to get water out of a cascading little stream.

There was plenty of wood for a healthy fire, and I treated myself to a double helping of freeze-dried spaghetti and a few cups of hot chocolate. I kept hearing little things skittering around among the underbrush, but I had no problems. The sky was sprinkled with stars; all else is black.

September 25

A snapping cold morning. My tight leg muscles began to loosen and stretch as I climbed up the ridge, away from the steep slopes of yesterday. The trail was hardly definable. The soil was so loose that it kept sliding down. Orangish-brown volcanic soil. Several views of the peaks flanking Nobel Canyon glowed yellow with the rising sun. Raymond Peak, around which I was skirting, rose ten thousand feet, the highest I've seen so far in California (except Shasta). I'm really getting into higher peaks.

Eagle Creek valley provided a surrealistic amphitheater to walk through. So many volcanic pinnacles surrounded the area, they

"Etiquette demanded that I stand off the trail."

looked like bristles of hair from a distance. Each about fifty feet high. A distant peak rose like a huge nub off its flat base — such a different landscape. I walked on through, finally stopping at Raymond Meadows for lunch. The sweet, earthy smell of a cow pasture surrounded me in this meadow, and I enjoyed a good lunch, bootless and reading Dostoevsky. I pushed on by Ebbetts Peak, across a road, and met a hairy, thin hiker coming the other way, who told of getting a couple of inches of snow several days ago. His girlfriend caught up, and we went our separate ways.

I topped out over Nobel Canyon, descended six hundred feet into the canyon, hopped a nice stream that came crashing down the steep slope, and trudged back up the other switchbacking side, out of the shadow of the ridge. The day wore on as I passed Nobel Lake, from which the stream crashed, and passed Tryon Peak at 9,200 feet at a pass devoid of vegetation taller than my knees. The wind was high at the pass, and here I crossed from

Toiyabe to Stanislaus national forests. As I began my downhill trot to find my campsite, a pack train of horses passed by. Etiquette demanded that I stand off the trail, and I hobbled down the steep slope, almost losing my balance. The horses almost panicked, with me below them, and began to kick rocks down. God, I hate horses on the trail, especially when their riders can't control them. At every pass I hope to see the high, jagged, granite peaks of the High Sierra, but no view here.

In the very last bit of light, I trotted down to Asa Lake. Soon all was black. A very peaceful evening. The lake was fed by numerous marshy springs, and in complete silence I filled my water bottles here. All one could hear was a faint tinkling of water. I felt like I could feel the same wariness a deer experiences when it cautiously lowers its head to drink. I could keep a nice fire crackling, but my exhausted shoulders and aching feet put me on to sleep. Some unknown rodent was scrambling around in my pack, but after I gave a few whacks with a stick, it left.

September 26

Another sky thick with clouds. The trail wasn't difficult, but a chilly wind blew across the small valleys I was traversing. The mountains are becoming more jagged and ominous, but they're still not obviously granitic, no outcrops. At one place the wind blew me almost completely off balance near a very steep slope.

Cloudy days are the most difficult. My favorite days back home were the cloudy ones. These are the days most of the world's population is indoors, out of the wind and by a fire. My memories of Christmas and Thanksgiving are utter heaven, and I sometimes fall into such a deep reverie, scratching my beard or moustache.

> *This has been one of those "homesick days," a day that is peculiarly empty — hollow, so to speak — when one talks, his voice sounds miles away. I worked hard*

all day, but after four o'clock my grasp
of what I was doing suddenly left me; the
bottom seemed to drop out of everything
so I quit! I wandered about aimlessly,
positively unable to fix my interest on
anything.

N. C. Wyeth, **The Wyeths**

Lunch went by quickly since it was a little chilly to sit still, so I put off reading more Dostoevsky until tomorrow. I left the lake's outlet, my lunch stop, and moved on. More miles to go. Just walk, let your mind wander, if you can think of something to think about, then hold onto it and think about it until you squeeze out every image or idea it might have. But think of something besides your feet, hips, or shoulders, or about how much farther you have to walk.

[Such a road] is wide enough, wide as the
thoughts it allows to visit you. Sometimes it
is some particular half-dozen rods which I
wish to find myself pacing over, as where
certain airs blow; then my life will come to
me, methinks; like a hunter I walk in wait
for it.

Henry David Thoreau
The Journal of Henry D. Thoreau

Then, one pass finally gave me a view of the beginnings of the High Sierra. It was beautiful but frightening. Blue rows of peaks, like teeth, created a jagged horizon, and myriads of snow patches in every crevice or cut dotted the view. I thought of walking through that by myself, with the chance of winter storms coming, and it scared me. But it also made me eager to get through quickly, hopefully to finish before the snows drove me out.

The winds drove most of the clouds away, producing a brisk, blue day. I descended to White Canyon, and my hurting feet and shoulders prodded me to stop. The light is dimmer in this canyon, so I thought it was later than it actually was. A bystander would have had a blast watching me try to hang my food: after a half hour of whining, anger, and work, I got the bag up. People had warned me of the bears in the Sierra and had said regarding my food, "Hang it or lose it." The bears weren't supposed to be bad until Sonora Peak, but that was only seven miles away. I finally had it hung over the river. The gurgling water played with my imagination, and I thought I could hear several bears walking in the river. After a dinner of instant potatoes, I was asleep.

September 27

Last night was surprisingly warm. Now, for the first time since the end of August, I unwound the gauze on my left big toe. The toe was still bald, but it didn't hurt excessively, so I just cleaned it a little and put on some antiseptic. I had just about everything ready to go when again it happened. I just broke down. The cold boots made my feet ache, and that unleashed a dam of anger and weariness and frustration. I cried and cried and cried, cursing every hated aspect of the hike.

But after five minutes of this, I became calm. The hike up the canyon was pleasant; when I let it all loose like that, I feel so peaceful afterwards, so rested. I can see things in better perspective, realizing that many of my fears about the distance and the coming cold weather don't need to be there. The top of the ridge cradled some bushes exhibiting fall colors, so I snapped a picture and soon came to the top of the pass by Sonora Peak. It was nice to look back and see peaks I had been rounding the days before. The trail continued to climb the flank of Sonora, up to the highest section of the trail so far on the hike, over ten thousand feet. I knew a road was near below, for I passed a couple of day hikers.

And the view was fantastic upon rounding Sonora Peak. I was getting a close-up of the snowy, jagged mountains I had seen yesterday. The added sensation of a terrific wind blowing around me heightened the thrill of the new section I was approaching.

I had lunch on the trail, out of the wind, and read a little. To my right, a huge silver coyote the size of a St. Bernard (may have been a wolf) jumped down the slope into a patch of trees. Never saw it again.

The trail descended about a thousand feet to the road. On the way down I talked to an older couple on a day hike. They strongly advised that I not continue. On Labor Day of this month several guys my age had frozen to death in the section I would be entering next week. I remember the lady saying, "I wouldn't go; you're too young; don't risk it." That scared me. As I approached the road, I must have gotten a little too much sun, or possibly I really was getting scared, for I suddenly became headachy, faint, and nauseous.

I began walking down the paved road, which was the temporary trail until another portion was complete. Forget this. A passing black pickup gave me a ride the few miles to a dirt road leading to the trailhead. At least I'm still on the trail. I began to feel better, and then a blue car with three young men inside offered a ride down the dirt road to the trail. Somehow we crammed my pack in, but soon the road became far too tortuous to drive on. So the four of us walked up back to the PCT, five miles from Sonora.

These guys are a delight, and they caught me up on the news of the civilized world. One was a blond, muscular Marine, always smiling and laughing. Another was a bearded, friendly, funny guy; and the third was a little out-of-shape, quiet, scientific type person. All three were engineers (I think) and were a joy to be around. They asked me to camp with them, and I gladly accepted. First time I'd camped with someone for two months!

The trail rounded Leavitt Lake, and I almost fell into its outlet in jumping across it. Then we began to climb and climb, up to the highest point yet on the PCT, the two-mile mark, 10,640 feet! Denny (the Marine) and I were far ahead of the other two, and the landscape around us was brown, devoid of any vegetation, with huge blotches of snow lying around us. The wind at the pass was tremendous and a real chiller. My hands and legs turned numb, but the view was absolutely glorious, one of the most memorable views yet and certainly the best since the Cascades. The sun was dropping fast and was casting a deep, lingering yellow on the landscape. But the mountains! How sheer the cliffs, how deep and sharp the valleys, as if God had fashioned them with a huge axe, cleaving the ground and splitting huge peaks. And they were granite. Denny told me, "And the views keep getting better; if I were you, I'd definitely keep going." Gazing upon this High Sierra spectacle was exciting, and yet these peaks weren't even close to being as high as the ones I'll be seeing in a couple of weeks.

Ken and Bob caught up, and soon we started down from the pass. The wide trail petered out into nothing after three-quarters of a mile. Ken handed us a block of chocolate, and we struck off downhill, cross-country. I remember thinking longingly of a hot bath as we trundled down. It's very cold.

Soon we found the trail and let our flashlights guide the way. It was cold and pitch black, but that added sound of human voices was so peaceful. We stopped at a creek to rest and soon made camp just off the trail. I went hunting for water for everyone, and for a treat I had a double helping of spaghetti. Also, Ken had some curry left over, which he let me finish up. But the company made such a difference. I could've hiked all night with those guys. We talked of nothing in particular, but an extended conversation meant so much. Soon we bundled up and rolled out the sleeping bags. A cloud cover passed over, and I pulled my tarp over me in case of rain, but all was fine. The stars are beautiful.

Walker Meadows to Campo

September 28

We awoke to a cold, clear blue morning. Getting started was a little slow as we all got our stuff together, but soon we were tromping on down Kennedy Canyon to Walker Meadows. I would hike with Ken and Bob for a while, then hike ahead and walk with Denny a while. I really felt like I was on vacation. Companionship put me in such peace of mind. I listened to Denny's stories of his experiences as a Marine, and I talked of my hike, plus everything one could imagine. Soon we were down to our shorts and T-shirts as the heat of the day grew.

We crossed a creek and took a longer break there than I ever would have taken alone, but I thoroughly enjoyed pouncing over boulders and sitting and listening to the rushing waters. In crossing a meadow we noted an unusual phenomenon: the ridge we were following became suddenly granitic, and one could see the exact line where volcanic mountains ended and granite mountains began.

We had lunch at the West Fork of the West Walker River, and the three gave me portions of beef stick, cheese, and Triscuits. I ate well that day. Unfortunately, our time together was almost over, for here they were going to stop. I lingered on, listening to Bob describe how at Stanford they were smashing deuterium embedded in glass with lasers.

I couldn't explain to them what a difference they had made for me and how they had encouraged me to go on through the High Sierra. But I tried to, and thanked them profusely, and took off, while they camped at Cinko Lake.

And what a change in terrain! Out of brown, volcanic soil, I was walking on granite shelves above shimmering lakes, with broad swaths of snow on the banks across the lakes. I can see why John Muir called these mountains "The Range of Light."

I could feel the hole left by leaving those three, and as I approached Dorothy Lake Pass, I met a long-haired, bearded ranger on a white horse. He was friendly, saying to his horse, "Just hold on, hold on; I'm just gonna talk to this hiker here." He gave me tips on the oncoming weather: "If it snows, just keep going. The snow may melt right up, but you'll be running into some Indian summer weather anyhow." He was such a funny character, named Crazy Larry. He described how he met his dog: "I was sitting in my cabin, havin' a few drinkie-winkies . . ." He'd even heard of Davidson.

But on again. The day was wearing on, so I had to tromp on by Dorothy Lake, past jagged, granite, snow-stuffed Forsyth Peak, and down across the Yosemite National Park border.

The trail paralleled Falls Creek, and huge Grace Meadow provided for a pretty, easy hike. The river was like a perfect canal winding through the meadow, a joy to sit next to. I had a candy bar by it. This country is also bear country, where I've heard all the horror stories for weeks about bears stealing food and ripping up tents.

I crossed the river and began looking for a tree with suitable branches to hang my food on. It's difficult to judge when the

"Just hold on, hold on; I'm just gonna talk to this hiker here."

sun will set in these canyons, so I just guessed by how far the shadow was up the far canyon wall. It was dark before I finally had my food properly counterweighted. I'm getting a little better at it, but it still takes a while. However, the night was uneventful, even though I constantly thought I was hearing bears creeping around the campsite.

September 29

Exactly one month after my birthday! That seems so long ago. Under a beautiful sky I moved down creek, following ducks whenever the trail disappeared over a slab of granite. Soon the sun warmed me up and I was in shorts and T-shirt. The trail was very distinct now that I was in Yosemite. Stream crossing was difficult though; they were broad and shallow, but inevitably I'd find a log or two to cross on. A break at Wilmer Lake. I couldn't help sighing in response to the tranquil beauty of this place with its granite cliffs surrounding the area and tall, cone-shaped, deep dark green pines. There were also raw patches on trees where bears had climbed to take the food of some hapless camper.

I began the first of a series of steep climbs up Bailey Ridge, ascending by a multitude of short switchbacks. The dark green forest, mingled with large granite shelves and boulders, provided a cool shade.

The trail leveled off, and I began climbing up Macomb Ridge. Such a tranquil hike. I thought of being home selling camping equipment at High Country. A curious note: when I'm deep in thought my heart, lungs, and legs all operate in time as I climb these canyons. These hills make the hike go by more quickly.

After a break on a boulder at the top of Macomb Ridge, I began the twelve-hundred foot descent into Stubblefield Canyon. The trail seemed nothing more than a stream bed, and after a long, knee-knocking descent, I came to the canyon floor. Here I had a nice lunch with my feet cooled in the creek, and read a few pages of Dostoevsky.

Back up again, eight hundred feet up another canyon. I'd pump my legs with my mind deep in thought until my heart was about to pound out of my chest, and then I'd take a short break and start again. This ridgetop afforded a beautiful view up Kerrick Canyon. Immense domes of creamy white granite reigned over the canyon. They were a little hazy, attesting to the great distance they were from me, but they still seemed so huge and close.

Back down again, another hour of boulder hopping downhill. My legs were getting quite a workout. I lost the trail for a moment by the sandy shores of the creek, but soon I picked it up again. And the colors! The aspens are turning golden. And every once in a while I'll see a splotch of yellow.

I began following the creek up towards its headwaters. A hiker passed by, and we talked for about ten minutes while he described the great fishing at Smedberg Lake. I continued on up, and soon the trail became lost under fallen trees. I found myself following deer trails and having to do some backtracking, but eventually I saw the trail and pushed on.

I camped by the creek that night in a sparsely treed meadow. After the usual half hour of heaving the rope over a high tree limb and hanging my food, I built a great campfire and fixed dinner. The wood was plentiful enough so that I could read by the fire for a while, a welcome friend as the night chill crept in. Fires are my best companions: they provide warmth, light, a little crackling and popping noise, and an almost hypnotic show of movement.

That night I awoke to a loud thunk near where I lay. Oh no, the bears are finally here. But no, I looked up to see a buck near my head. That was an unforgettable sight, his large body and thin legs silhouetted by a waning moon, and a head that would silently dip as he nibbled along the ground. As I reached for my glasses in my boots to get a better look, he heard me and sprang away.

September 30

Another cold, clear morning. The day began with a climb up to Seavey Pass, and at the pass I changed into shorts and T-shirt. On the way down I was again in deep thought, scratching my beard and staring at the ground in front of me. I looked up to see myself surrounded by deer! I had quietly blundered into the middle of a herd! Once they realized that I had noticed them, they slowly began to move away; but I had time to drop my pack and get a picture of a doe picking its way among some boulders.

The trail began to traverse down the ridge, down its typically steep, bouldery stream bed, as granite domes rose on three sides. I was surrounded by giants which seemed to loom above, uncaring of this little pink body stepping around among them. Near Benson Lake, among tall grass, I took a break before attempting to cross Piute Creek. I got across but found myself straddling a log amidst a maze of fallen logs. After about twenty minutes I slipped and climbed my way out of that pile. Ferns now turning golden and orange due to the cooler weather covered the ground.

I climbed on up yet another canyon, up the myriad of short switchbacks. Lunch was taken beside a rushing creek, just sitting on a boulder, soaking up warmth from the rock and the sun. On up. Volunteer Peak rocketed straight up a thousand feet. I stood in awe of so much rock reared up before me, the greatest yet of the regal giants standing in this land. The trail made truly enigmatic turns as it then dropped quickly down four hundred feet and then climbed right back up again. I passed by rockbound Smedberg Lake, pausing to admire its beautiful canal-like inlet creek.

Up again. I looked down on a meadow, like a football field, with ribbons of water imbedded in it working their way to the lake. During a pause in the steep ascent, I washed the sticky grime off my legs and arms; and with this refreshing break, I crossed another meadow to see Benson Pass in a cut in the ridge above. Up one more time, and my major goal of the day was obtained at this windy, bare, sandy pass. The steep canyon below blocked out most views, so with aching feet I descended back out of the sun to the cool shadows of this valley. On the way down, I caught a glimpse of a distant ridge, a saw-tooth line of vast granite spikes

— the mountains to come. They were red, bathed in the light of the setting sun.

Wilson Creek was a world of its own, with pines and firs and a stream bubbling by me, all in a half-light. Numerous potential campsites dotted the shores, but I pushed on down in order to set myself up to be able to get to Tuolumne tomorrow. Tuolumne — that word held a special kind of magic for me, being the start of the last section of high mountains before the Mojave Desert. I'll be *so* close to home then.

In the Matterhorn Canyon I again hung my food as all light faded away and had supper in bed. A daddy longlegs kept getting in my hot chocolate. I set up a little candle instead of building a fire and was secure in my small hemisphere of light, nothing at all visible beyond it. The air was so still; not a sound on the bottom of this vast canyon.

October 1

The first day of October and the day of arrival at Tuolumne! That idea picked me up and made me stuff down breakfast quickly. The floor of Matterhorn Canyon was encrusted with frost, and this forest flanked on either side by vast granite walls was still in a half-light of morning. I needed to stamp my feet to get the feeling in them, and to rub my hands together constantly.

Light hit the top of the western canyon wall. Soon, however, I was climbing up the eastern wall, up a thousand feet, puffing fog the whole way. As I climbed the sun worked its way down the opposite wall, and soon I had an aerial sunlit view of Matterhorn Peak and other ridges. They looked stark and hard, just vast spikes of granite.

I must have begun early, for it took several miles before I began to warm up enough to take off my mittens and sweater. The hike went fast and was really enjoyable. The trees would allow me to see a flash of granite cliff on the horizon every so often, and several broad streams made for exciting boulder hops across their waters. Virginia Canyon was particularly beautiful, as the water had sculpted round, smooth shapes in the rock and then gone sliding over a cliff, down into distant valleys. I took a break here and enjoyed testing my balance by jumping among the boulders.

Another uphill, where I met a striking, red-bearded hiker with piercing eyes and his red hair wound in a long pigtail. He called himself Strider, and we had a short talk. He said Indian summer was here, but that I was definitely cutting it close with the coming winter storms.

This didn't keep me from enjoying a good lunch by Cold Canyon creek five miles later. I washed off more grime, read a little, and enjoyed the warm sun in this open, broad meadow here. The peaks of the John Muir Trail and the beginning of the highest mountains yet stood erect on the horizon: the Cockscomb, Unicorn Peak, and Cathedral Peak.

Back in the forest, the trail took me on downhill until I began to hear a distant roar. Oh, Lord! Across Cold Canyon was a huge, glittering waterfall straight from the rock of the opposite wall down to the river below. Here, at the Glen Aulin High Sierra Camp, there were several backpackers, all clustered in these camps at the bottom of Cold Canyon. But what a paradise. Another waterfall made its presence known as it crashed down several granite shelves. This was Tuolumne Falls. I talked to a lone girl hiker for a couple of minutes and crossed the Tuolumne River. Several hikers passed by, saying, "You have a long hike if you want to get to the road tonight." But the excitement of this paradise, the nearing of the conclusion of this section, and seeing people again kept me quickly pushing on those last six miles.

At the top of the Falls, I could look back and see all the huge, white granite world that river was crashing and sliding down to.

The last stretch was level, and Tuolumne Meadows provided tranquil scenery as I walked over rock slabs and yellow meadow. My feet began to ache badly as I neared the conclusion of the day's hike; and the light kept dimming until darkness had almost completely closed in by the time I arrived at Tioga Road.

I stopped for a moment to inspect the tiny Soda Springs, a carbonated spring. Across the meadow, next to the road, stood a man and woman wrapped in bulky down coats and caps. I must have been a queer sight walking across the grass in shorts and long-sleeved wool shirt. I asked them for a ride, and they consented to giving me a ride to Lee Vining. What a blessing; I'd hate to have to try to hitchhike to that food drop in the dark. They were from Switzerland, and we visited as we descended out of the mountains. The night air must have been very cold, for the warmth of the car seeping into my skin made it tingle, and I sank deep into the seat enjoying the rest with nothing on my back. We kept going down and down, until the black outlines of mountains were behind us and a straight horizon was below. That was quite a shock, seeing that flat land of Mono Basin, although I could see no details since all was black.

In Lee Vining the couple dropped me off at the market, and I thanked them very much. I bought some milk and sweet rolls at the market and sat out in front on a bench — back in the white lights of civilization with cars passing and with strange faces and voices. At a hotel a man said I could camp at the county playground for the night, and after walking down the main street for a while and visiting a campaign headquarters for saving Mono Lake, I made a dark trek down a side street until I came to the playground. Here I made an uneasy camp (I'm so unused to having voices anywhere near), and every ten minutes or so I hear something; there's also a constant hum of activity in a town. But I was excited at having made it here: in Oregon I never could have imagined being this far along. I felt I had come a long way, especially when I looked out and saw the straight horizon of Mono Basin below. The sky was full of stars, and I soon dozed off.

October 2

Another clear day. After some breakfast I carried my pack over to a restroom and spent an hour washing up. Some guys were getting ready to start sprinkling the grass in the park, so I moved on out. My first stop was the laundromat, where I sat half clothed while most of my clothes were being washed, and then I dressed into that half while the other half washed. I wrote Mom and Dad and Ruth and Karrie[35] and read some Dostoevsky. The box at the P.O. was wonderful, as always, and I sat in front of the Lee Vining Market reading letters from Gia, Liza, Anne,[36] Mom and Dad, John Hartman, and that distant place somewhere back east, Davidson College. Back to the P.O. to mail letters, back to the market to buy over fifty dollars of food to carry me through the Sierra. I had trouble carrying the grocery bags out, and an old man carried one for me. Some people are truly kind. I spoke to practically no one though; I guess I'm tired of talking about the hike.

It took me a couple of hours to pack up. God, it's heavy! With eighty pounds, I staggered out of the park. I just kept saying to myself, this is the last time I'll have to do this; all the future sections will be short; just get through this. At a camping store I was able to get some white gas, thanks to a woman who let me buy a single quart from a half-gallon can.

Out of here! Lee Vining was nice, but my desire to get going and not to feel so conspicuous made me eager to leave. The sun was lowering, and I still had to get to Tuolumne. I made the mile to a ranger station, where I walked up on a guy my age working on a truck. We began to talk, and he allowed me to use the station phone. He's a very considerate guy; he let me have some cookies. The call home was a heart-puller. Mom and Dad seemed so far away, and this was the last time I'd talk to them for over three weeks. Their concern about winter storms was evident, and I promised I'd drop out of the higher mountains if I did meet treacherous weather. When I hung up, a hole seemed to hang in me as I sat in this wooden garage. Home is nearer than ever, yet so far. My pack, newly laden, was now a curse with its great weight. The guy returned and led me to a campsite behind the station where I could stay for the night. So much for Tuolumne. He was very giving and had hiked what I was getting ready to hike, but not with one packload. He gave me his number to call when I arrived at Weldon so the Forest Service could keep tabs on me in case something happened. I thanked him profusely for his information, time, and friendliness; and in the dark I ate a can of salmon that Mom had sent. Tomorrow I was starting the attempt to hike 312 miles with an eighty-pound pack over the roughest, highest, most remote trail yet, and with the threat of oncoming winter. Why am I doing this to myself?

October 3

As has always seemed to be the case in the past, my fellow man pulled me out of this fear and gave me the push to continue. I packed out of the ranger station in the first light of morning and began walking up the road back to the trail at Tuolumne. The air was cold, as the sun hadn't reached down past the tops of the mountains yet. Soon a man stopped and gave me a ride to the meadows, where I had left off. He was very kind, and we had a good conversation. He hated me calling him "sir"; he said, "What am I, your grandfather or something?" That's a southeastern convention that's stuck with me.

The day promised to be a beautiful blue as we arrived at the trailhead. A ranger said we'd have to hang our food due to bears, and some minutes later, I was off. I began the long ten-mile hike down Lyell Canyon, an immense canyon with a flat floor of meadows and stands of trees. Soon I was in shorts, and little flies kept biting my legs. I haven't had trouble with insects in a long time. Hiking was easy and slow; the heavy pack made me stop for a rest every two miles or so. When I stopped for a lunch of cheese and tortilla (a new idea I'm trying; it's tough and easily packed), the man who had given me a ride caught up and stopped to talk. We said our last goodbye when he left to climb up the ridge to his camp for a weekend stay.

As the day wore on the trail began to slant upwards as it neared the root of this long canyon. Two guys named Rick and Bob passed me, and soon I found we kept passing each other, so we decided to go ahead and camp in the same spot. I had hoped to be able to hike farther, but the promise of companionship pressed me to stay. I'm so glad I did. Bob was an older man in his fifties, Rick in his mid twenties. Rick had biked across the country, and we talked about that. They helped me hang my food with Rick perched on my shoulders as he tried to push the sack up into a tree; and soon we began wobbling around — Rick waving his arms and me staggering, which sent Bob into laughing hysterics. After dinner we sat around the fire telling bear stories until we fell into a peaceful silence, our eyes staring at the hissing embers. Their presence made the night a holiday.

October 4

Well, no thumping sound of a creeping bear met my ears last night, and the first thing I did was to look up and see my food bags hanging safely in the tree. I had so much food that it took me half an hour to rearrange the pack. But I'm out of Yosemite, and today we'll climb a high pass that supposedly few Yosemite bears cross. I can't believe that I heard all those horror stories about bears and I never even saw one.

The trail wound on up the headwaters of the Tuolumne River, and the three of us talked periodically, mostly just rubbed our hands together, waiting for the sun to come over the ridge. We came out upon a small open glade with a green alpine pond nestled in its center. But we're above the trees at an altitude where just grass and granite exist. We took a few pictures and then began to ascend a granite ridge. We talked about everything: Andrew Wyeth, writing (Bob's hobby is writing), John Muir, and soon they began talking of their work in Pasadena, and I forged

Walker Meadows to Campo/173

ahead a little. Donohue Pass, at 11,056 feet, my highest yet, opened in front of me, and I could see all of the Minarets. A haze from a forest fire below filled the landscape, so much was not visible, but Banner Peak and Mt. Ritter careened out of the rock south of me. Snow-gutted Mt. Lyell and the Cathedral Range formed a vast jagged wall to my right, the gateway to the highest of the High Sierra; and to the left, miles and miles away, the mountains made a sheer drop down to the Owens Valley. It was fairly chilly up here, and I had the unpleasant prospect of finding a place to relieve myself on a ridge of jumbled granite.

Down we went, two thousand feet back into some sparse trees. This weight on my back really exhausts me, especially on descents; it's like going down large steps, so Rick and Bob were fairly far ahead until I caught up at Island Pass. We had had lunch at Rush Creek earlier, where we had met a group of hikers going the other way. Bob said, "And this is Tom; he's hiking to Mexico and has three brothers and three sisters, all of whom are doctors." Apparently I had been rambling on to him about my family, and this presentation made me laugh. One guy tried to lift my pack. He looked at me as if I was crazy, and they moved on.

But here at Island Pass I found a nice rock to sit on while we all took pictures near a crystal clear, boulder strewn lake. The day was wearing on, and Bob and Rick had to veer off the trail to the base of Mt. Ritter, which they were going to climb tomorrow. I had enjoyed their company so much it really hurt to see them go. I felt like following them over there. But with a few words and handshakes we departed. I guess it's best. I walked on downhill, and looked back over Thousand Island Lake, shining in a setting sun, and fancied that I could see them walking among the boulders there.

But now I had a decision to make. I could hike the prettier but more difficult John Muir Trail for the next five miles, or hike near the easier but incomplete PCT. Choosing the latter, I pushed on down the beginning of the San Joaquin River. To the east was San Joaquin Mountain, with the Two Teats next to it, all crowning a bare, massive ridge, which was a dull pink-grey in the setting sun. The trail was easy, but aching feet put a stop to the day's hike; I had made little mileage today and attributed it to the pack. Despite a little uneasiness about bears, I slept with my head against my pack. It's so quiet.

October 5

It's a cold morning, this third day in the High Sierra. Two things I can see are going to be real problems. I had bought Grape Nuts cereal to eat for breakfast, and already I'm sick of the taste. I have to force it down. Also, mice have gotten in my pack. After some complaining, I rebagged the spilled food and got started.

To my right were sheer vertical granite walls flanking the San Joaquin River canyon with ribbons of water from the lakes along the John Muir Trail above me free-falling through cracks and thundering on the rocks below. Soon the trail went up, and I changed into shorts near a grassy creek. Another blue, warm day. I began to approach a road, and, sure enough, I met a lot of day hikers, every one of whom said, "That's quite a load, isn't it?" with a laugh.

On a huge wooden bridge near the road, I had lunch with the San Joaquin River splashing below. It was nice to follow this friend, but after that lunch, with some reading of Dostoevsky, I shouldered my pack with a groan and moved on.

Soon I came to a detour to the Devils Postpile Monument. I had been waiting to see this for a long time (two years), and so I hid my pack under some leaves and trotted the mile down. I feel so thin and light without the pack, like someone is pushing me from behind.

To my frustration, I found there was no longer a bridge across the river; so, after much deliberation, I resigned myself to slogging across the deep, broad river. I drew many stares, squishing up to the Postpile, for there was a road nearby and people were there. The pictures I got made the trip worth the effort. The perfect hexagonal posts, formed by cooling andesite, impressed me as being a true miracle of nature. The top of the hill has been polished smooth by a glacier and looks like bathroom tile.

Back to my pack, where I met a husband and wife couple. Great! the trail I took to the Postpile is *the* trail, but to avoid sloshing across that river a third time, I detoured on a newly cleared trail. The promise of a campground with hot springs in a mile or so prompted me to stop after only twelve miles. I need to check out my left toe anyway. I read a lot of Dostoevsky until the sun dipped, and then made dinner in the dark, with other hikers' campfires here and there around me. I felt no urge to talk to anyone; I guess the disappointment in little mileage makes me want to get to sleep early in order to make miles in the morning. But to be able to sit and read and let my mind constructively play with a story is such a refreshing break. No hot springs though. Well, good night.

October 6

I started out in the gray of the morning, just as the sun began to thaw the air and ground. The trail began its slow ascent up Mammoth Mountain, up sixteen hundred feet. The Minarets were visible, stabbing the sky behind and north of me. I came upon a small warm spring with a fine lace of algae swirled around its source. The sun began to warm me up as I passed the Red Cones — two bald, rounded red hills, true to their names. On up to a flat, yellow meadow, where I dropped my pack to share lunch with a few ants. I read a little and started off again. This pace is wearing on me. I sat down once and went into a dream-like rest and almost fell asleep sitting up. I'm *so* tired. This pack is really too heavy; I can't believe I'm trying to bring this much. And the trail — straight up and straight down, all day long. I think I drank some bad water at Tuolumne, for I hate to even think about eating, and the diarrhea is bad again. I went deep into thought as I completed the long, long traverse up to ten thousand feet on the ridge overlooking Cascade Valley. Silver Pass, another long-awaited landmark, was visible ahead. The far end of this long canyon was crowned with a vast ridge of tumbled yellowish-gray granite. The cliff above the pass reminded me of the inside of a heart. Glaciers had pulled huge shards of rock away from the face of the cliff, leaving long thick ridges and bands running vertically down. But the pass was still many miles away, and the sun was dipping low. I groaned on. At Duck Lake's outlet, between two high walls of granite, I enjoyed a candy bar. The ridge was becoming dangerously steep, so the trail ran high up on the ridge, weaving its way among chiseled rock and tumbled mounds of stone.

As the sky's darkness began to push the sun behind the horizon, I finally came upon Purple Lake, one side of which was filled with scree. Apparently the cliff beside it had caved in.

I tried to break sticks for a fire, but my shoulders were so exhausted that I couldn't even stand up straight, much less collect firewood. So I started a little blaze to cook macaroni and cheese. For some reason all this food tastes horrible; I really almost want to throw it back up.

I didn't get much sleep tonight; mice were attacking my pack. I could even catch them with my flashlight peeking around my pack, but knock around as much as I might, I'd still hear them five minutes later ripping holes in my food bags. I'd picture powdered milk spilling all over the inside of the pack, and then I'd get furious. These guys just won't quit.

October 7

I pulled myself out of the bag and started away under another light sky, which was just beginning to receive the sun's warmth. A climb up a virtual spiral staircase of rock put me on top of the ridge again, and soon I was walking between two shattered cliffs on a trail made of piles of blasted stone. At Lake Virginia I sat on a mat of stubby grass surrounding the water and could survey the peaks serrating the horizon. A constant cool wind blows here and makes the water lap on the edges of the lake. It's very quiet.

Fatigue, or languidness, was already seeping back into me as I descended eight hundred feet to Tully Hole, a meadow oasis in the midst of this severe stone world. The meadow was laced with deep creeks sliding down from the nearby cliffs. I noticed a Starflite tent, just like the one I had lost so long ago, perched by a tree at the meadow's edge. After a short break, I trundled down into forest, crossed Fish Creek on a large, sturdy new bridge, and began the long ascent up to Silver Pass, a sixteen hundred-foot climb. The trail made short, quick switchbacks by a steep, crashing stream, and here I had some lunch. Eating is still a mechanized action; I just look forward to being able to sit for a while.

Then the owner of the tent strode down. He was a writer for some newspaper in Arizona, a bearded, young guy, and we talked for a while. But the day's waiting miles gnawed on me until I got going again. Meeting him was a welcome break.

Silver Pass was a series of granite ledges, and at the east ledge I came upon yet another one to climb. Up past the realm of the trees, up to where only grass grew around the Lake of the Lone Indian, and then the trail climbed a ledge behind it. I stopped frequently to rest, but the brisk wind would cool me enough to keep me going. And the sun is incredibly bright; I find myself squinting a lot. To the north, the Minarets were visible in the distance, standing at the far end of Cascade Valley.

Then I came to the pass, and icy snow had filled it. I kicked steps up the slope, as memories of Washington flooded back whenever my boots crunched through. I fell to my knees a couple of times, but eventually I popped over the top. The mountains I saw were more massive and serene than spectacular, particularly one that looked like a warped, tilted tabletop, far to the south. The wind pushing through the pass urged me to move on down, back down clacking shards of rock, past Silver Pass Lake. One tree, gnarled and split, held on by that lake. I figured there were probably mice even up here. The clear, quiet day was coming to a close as I again entered trees, and I even met one or two mosquitoes while crossing marshy Pocket Meadow.

The trail made switchbacks down a very steep eight hundred-foot high cliff. To my left was another huge wall, also eight hundred feet high, of pure smooth granite. Earlier streams had fashioned the wall into kind of an amphitheater, but now just one hairline of water dropped in a free fall, drifting all the way down to an echoing trickle at the bottom. The light was now quite dim, so I hurried down until the trickle had become a more sizeable stream.

Wow! There was a perfect spot for a campsite, with pre-chopped firewood and a few cardboard boxes. I guess some trail builders had passed through here recently. I restrained nothing in building a good, warm fire which made the nauseating macaroni and cheese a little more palatable. I decided to try to hang my entire pack on a small nearby tree; and I laid out my sleeping bag far from it, so that if any mice did get in, I wouldn't be able to hear them and would maybe get some sleep tonight.

October 8

I descended on the trail into deeper canyons to begin today's climb, twelve hundred feet up into Bear Creek to begin the next pass. Every day I just aim for a pass and try to get over it and try to set myself up for a good position for the next day's pass. I was now hiking in aspens, which still retained a few golden leaves, but many more leaves were strewn on the ground. Then a vibrating clap impacted the ground, like a dull explosion: trail builders blasting rock. I walked by them and spoke a few words to one of the organizers. He was a friendly man who spoke of recent snow flurries on Silver Pass. This made me aware of what a thin line I was walking on; I'm just in a delicate Indian summer which can any day give way to winter storms.

But now under a blue sunny sky, I crossed Quail Meadows and began the twenty switchbacks of the climb up Bear Ridge. The Vermillion Cliffs were visible across the precipitous canyon through a thick lodgepole pine forest, a display of granite turrets and spires. As I neared the top I became more and more languid. I stopped for lunch, but the food had to be forced down again. What is wrong with me? I feel so nauseous all the time. I laid back on the trail to rest and began forming in my mind what I would write to my parents. The difficult things are so different from what I thought they would be — mice in my food, fatigue, sickness…. It's ironic that the weather is fine. I dragged on over the ridge, my stomach feeling like it's full of air. Food just gives me an unpleasant bloated feeling.

As I began my way up Bear Creek, I met an older couple hiking by who were from San Francisco. When I saw their arms and legs, I realized how filthy mine have gotten. I look almost black compared to them. The man told me that a snowstorm was expected to pass through in three days.

I pushed on a few more miles after they turned off to their campsite. The trail is now weaving over rock slabs, indicative of the increase in elevation. I found a campsite which looked like it had been well used over the summer, so I knew there would be lots of rodents around. Now my food fits in my sleeping bag sack, so I was able to hang just it filled with food and leave my pack on the ground. Bear Creek is nearby, providing a pleasant background murmur.

October 9

No mouse or chipmunk problems last night. My aching feet eventually warmed up my boots, and hiking was pleasant as I moved slowly uphill among boulders and ledges and sparse trees. I thought a lot of being close to Mexico and of being able to go home.

The terrain became increasingly bare as I neared Selden Pass. These days go by quickly: I get up, the sun climbs up the sky; I eat lunch, the sun is above me; I hike some more, the sun sets; I sleep — and then the cycle begins again. I really feel like I'm living in a cyclic, constantly repeating universe, with the day at its barest essentials. I simply watch it go by as I hike; there is nothing to provide mental concentration except my book — which I drink in at every lunch — and having to set my mind on getting over the next pass.

Selden Pass was a jewel nestled among the severe ridges of the Sierra Nevada. From the bare stone pass I could look back and see Marie Lake, which displayed a palette of various deep blues. Coming to a pass is like climbing out of a labyrinth for a moment and looking around before descending into the next canyon. I can see mountains and cliffs not visible from below, and a whole new world opens up.

After lunch at one of the quietly lapping Sally Keyes Lakes, I descended through a meadow and on down again into forest. I experienced a stomach ache on the way down and took an antacid tablet, but that and the wrapping for my big toe are the only items from my first aid kit I've used during this entire hike. The day ended at Piute Creek, where I hung my food high by a huge pine in the half-light. My emotions have become so childlike. When I have trouble hanging the food, I get mad and start wimpering and yelling. There's no one around to keep this from, and in a way it's a release from all the frustrations of the day. Afterwards I feel relaxed and calm, although a little ashamed. I talked to no one today. It makes a differernce; all this space yet no people.

My bitterness evaporated, and the only
resentment I felt was concentrated on
myself. I lay there a long time, sobbing,
"What a pity, what an infinite pity!" So
my pride was gone as well. A Virginian, I
was brought up to believe that a
gentleman never gives way to his feelings.
I felt no shame then, although I do now.

Richard E. Byrd, **Alone**

The mice are rampant tonight. I framed a few with the beam from my flashlight, but I couldn't fling a rock fast enough to nab one. The sky is beautiful.

October 10

Mice got into my food last night. The cheese has numerous minute furrows where their teeth gnawed away. I followed up the large South Fork of the San Joaquin River, where I stopped to wash off the gummy black grime on my arms, hands, and legs. I feel so light without the pack, and my skin tingles with life when I wash off. The slope I was traversing was rocky and steep; but soon I entered a straight, soft path under arches of pine boughs, which gave the trail a dark, misty, mysterious quality.

With home the center of my thoughts, I turned up Evolution Creek, confronting a loud, splashing torrent of water leaping from granite bowl to granite bowl down to its confluence with the San Joaquin. Such a bright morning, I had to stop to rest and take this place in.

Then up to the calmer, broader headwaters. I had to cross somewhere up here, and I tried to maneuver a few huge logs over the stream. I'd stand one up on end and give it a push, succeeding only in dashing myself with a wave of water as I watched the log float away downstream. At this time a hiker came crashing by through the trees, and we stopped to talk. Heck, I might as well eat lunch too.

We talked about equipment and the surrounding terrain, and he said I could cross upstream a ways. We parted, and a mile upstream the river narrowed, which meant it was also moving faster. I had to practically close my eyes and run, and after a few spine-thrilling, stomach-shocking wavers on the log, I crossed successfully. The trail was making its climb up to long-awaited Muir Pass as the trees became sparse and the meadows more broad.

At a bend in the trail stood an old man in nothing but a white undershirt, khaki shorts, and sandals. He had a long, bushy white beard and no hair. "Hello," he said. "You must be hiking from Canada." I guess it was obvious: dirty, suntanned, large pack, bent shoulders, and a shirt with its shoulders worn away from the pack straps. I said yes, and he invited me up to his cabin.

A beautiful, thin Swedish girl with long brown hair was washing dishes at a wooden table outside a one-room cabin. Turned out this guy was a ranger, and this girl was his assistant. She invited me in for blueberry muffins and tea. He tried to call another ranger by a small radio, so I could have rangers watching for me on this next section, but the radio just whined and screeched; he couldn't get through. He warned me of a storm which was going to pass through soon. He also gave me a letter to give to another ranger down the trail, so I was dubbed the High Sierra Courier. Since they were going to be helicoptered out before the storms hit, they had lots of leftover food to give me, which I gratefully accepted. This meeting was so uplifting to my spirit. I left after a handshake and a hug and began plodding across a marshy meadow, again riding on the push that two kind people had given me.

The time I had spent there ate up several miles, but I didn't care too much. I climbed up a thousand feet, where no trees could eke survival from the thin layer of stubby grass-covered soil on granite. I rolled out my bag by a still lake. At eleven thousand feet, this was the highest yet I had camped. The ranger had given me an orange, which I devoured for dessert. The stars would be beautiful tonight, but I fell asleep as they began to appear.

October 11

The sky was a deep blue, but the sun hadn't yet appeared over the bare granite peaks to warm things up. My tarp crackled under a thin sheet of ice formed from my condensed breath. Putting on my boots was painful, and I had to thaw them out on my feet.

But the feet began to warm up and stop aching as I went and as the sun flooded the canyon with light. There were no trees up here, just patches of stubby yellow grass that could live among the broken rock and wide shelves of granite. I lost the trail for a moment as it wove unseen over a rock slab, but soon I found it again. It climbed a thousand feet but took five miles to do so. The whole terrain had an air of newborn sterility. Sunlight flashed off heaps and piles and hollows of broken white granite, and the trail was very amorphous; I boulder hopped most of the way. Wanda Lake and Lake McDermand sat in depressions in the rock, like crystal blue ponds filling a moon crater. This area looked like it must have looked ten thousand years ago when it was scraped bare by glaciers.

I plodded up the slow incline towards the pass, where the air was disquietingly still and the world completely silent — all except for my stomach, which growled and churned at the thought of a roast beef sandwich.

The pass (Muir Pass, 11,955 feet) was overshadowed by close, high cliffs, so the view wasn't astounding, but the moon-like quality of this place was enough. Muir hut, a round, conical hut made of granite, sat there as if to say, "What are you doing here?" I walked into the cubicle, which had stone benches lining the wall, and found a piece of paper on one of the benches. I couldn't believe it. It was a note from Penny and Bill! They said they had camped here just three days ago and were going to wait for me at Weldon for a day to see if I would show up. I read and reread the note in complete disbelief; what an unexpected turn of events! They were the last two people I expected to hear from, especially here. The note ended, ". . . don't camp here; there's a mouse living in the hut, and he may get in your pack." So the mice are even up here.

I ate lunch in the hut as tufts of wind began thudding against it like dull, distant explosions. As I started down from the pass, I looked back to see a wall of clouds on the horizon. So they finally got here; the Indian summer is over.

I stopped for water at glacier-fed Helen Lake, where the water was so cold it gave me a headache. As I descended from around the flanks of the Black Giant, rows upon rows of vertical, vast spikes stood like sentinels. Among those jagged ridges were peaks of the Palisades group, close to the highest points in the Continental U.S. I moved on down to the labyrinth of canyons at the base of these walls, back to the world of grass, and eventually back to the trees. A thick, deep swath of ice covered part of the trail, making for a frightening, quick traverse over a steep ridge. Down, down, down, until the unseen peaks above blocked out the sun.

The descent seemed to last forever, but without a break I moved on. The wind was beginning to pick up, and I relished the thought of meeting the ranger to whom I was to bring this letter that the past ranger had given me. The light of day almost gone, but I could see his cabin; a strange thumping was coming out of it. He was playing the drums. I knocked twice and, obviously a little embarrassed, he gladly accepted the letter; but he offered no invitation to come inside. I was a little angry, but I had to remember it's his prerogative to ask me in or not, not his duty. So I camped a half mile away, by the trail, saddened by the chill air and the anticipated but unreceived invitation to stay in a cabin.

October 12

It's happened. My heart sank as I saw a thin lace of white spread over the brown of pine needles on the forest floor and a silent whispering of white snowflakes floating around me. The next pass is the highest yet, so I decided to take it easy today.

So agreed the ranger, who came crunching out to my tarp and looked under it to talk to me. He suggested that tonight I camp below Mather Pass instead of trying to get over it. "It's a mother, and if you try to go over it in a storm, your hands will go numb, you won't be able to set up your tarp, and then you're screwed." So after reading some I struck out. The sky was low and gray, but periodically a brighter patch of sky would show itself. LeConte Canyon was one of the most spectacular canyons yet, with vertical two thousand-foot-high white granite cliffs on either side. The canyon floor was forest except where massive rockslides had created havoc and obliterated stands of trees. I passed an older man on his way to ask the ranger how he could get out of these mountains before more bad weather came.

A brisk wind cleared up the sky almost completely, however, and I had a lunch of banana chips (from the first ranger) and nuts. The Citadel, a cluster of boulders the size of high rise office buildings, rose poised above me. Here I began the climb up Palisade Creek towards Mather Pass, meeting two hikers who had gotten caught at the pass by snow yesterday. The only thing they had found difficult was visibility and strong winds; that was encouraging. I just have four more passes to clear before I'm out of the High Sierra, but it seems as if the weather makes progress slower and slower the farther along I get.

I camped at the last stand of trees before the tree line, and paid a lot of attention to rigging up a strong shelter with my tarp.

The sky is almost cloud-free, but I don't trust the weather enough to try to get over the pass today.

October 13

A painfully cold morning. I had slept with my boots to avoid the unpleasant thawing out process, but I still needed some hot coffee and a fire before I could warm up.

The sky was a yellow-blue when I awoke, so I began to climb towards Mather Pass; but clouds began sliding over me. God, it's cold. The wind, as always, is constantly whispering around me. The day began with the Golden Staircase, a nearly vertical climb of numerous short switchbacks, and the terrain's aspect changed from taiga[37] to arctic alpine. At the top of the staircase I could look back and see terrain I'd covered on yesterday's hike, back to where I had lunch under the Citadel. All the surrounding spikes of mountains were covered with a spider web of white snow from the day before.

What magnificent desolation. I walked on spongy, stubby grass which could cling only at the edges of gray Palisade Lakes. Smooth granite walls rose on either side of me, all capped by a ceiling of gray clouds. The clouds were formless, as if a blanket of solid gray had been pulled over the terrain. And the whispering wind, stronger now, still echoed as it funneled through this basin. A light snow began drifting down, lightly stinging the skin as it landed on my face; a world of granite, snow, and water.

But as I trudged on, I heard a faint ticking sound near my feet. There was a tiny bird, puffed into a ball the size of an egg, pecking on a solid rock. What a tough guy. I knelt down right next to it to watch, and it didn't mind me a bit. Eventually it flew away; but that tiny, soft ball of life was an inspiration.

Now I could see Mather Pass. It was merely a small notch at the top of a vast twelve hundred-foot-high wall, a wall that scarcely

"I heard a faint ticking sound near my feet."

bore a trail. I walked among a great upheaval of rock, a few stones pushed to the side indicating the trail. A surprise at the pass! The clouds dissipated after squeezing over the ridge, so I met a cold yellow sun and blue sky. But the wind was tremendous, and I had a frantic moment when I thought the wind had blown away a mitten. Not a real big deal, but I dearly loved the few things I had with me, and I threw myself into another rampage. I've got to get a hold on myself and stop letting my emotions break like that. Here at 12,100 feet a whole new leg of the John Muir Trail opened before me, and I left the last leg behind as I began the descent. Lakes dotted a meadow below, like craters in a field, and here I ate lunch, lying down with my pack propped up beside me to block the constant wind. I felt so depleted; the sun is cold but harsh, the wind is constant, the air is thin, and again I'm in a languid, empty state.

I plodded down the rest of the two thousand-foot descent to begin tomorrow's climb. But the trail seemed to take a wrong turn, and after checking the maps and exploring the Kings River a little, I found that I was royally lost. So with this unpleasant discovery, I made camp and built a huge fire. A tidal wave of clouds began streaming out of the canyon from Mather Pass, so I wrapped up in my tarp and thermal blanket as well as my sleeping bag.

October 14

The sky is gray again, but the clouds, having dropped, now swirl about the lower peaks and hills. I set off to follow the trail I was on, hoping it would take me to a vantage point where I could work my way back to the PCT. I began to veer back to an alpine meadow where I thought the trail was located. Everything was frosted silver due to a freezing short rain last night. Grass crackled and crunched underfoot, and periodically the clouds would diffuse and a patch of yellow would glow through the gray ceiling, lighting up the snapping cold terrain in a misty shine. It's so quiet and cold; nothing is stirring. And huge, ghost-like clouds sprawl and tumble by in complete silence. My ears almost rang it was so quiet.

I moved on back west again, and eventually stumbled across the trail. Up I went towards Pinchot Pass. The clouds were very thick now, and I stepped over streams which gurgled under thin sheets of ice. Some I could walk right over.

Then the snow came — pleasantly at first, until the wind whipped it up. I put on everything, even my rain gear, which cut out the biting wind. As I climbed towards Pinchot Pass, away from grass and all life, the clouds closed in. The snow now blew by horizontally. I lost all sense of where I was and just plodded along, following the trail of rock. When the trail sloped to an even grade and then began to drop, and when the wind force grew to a whining push against me, I knew I was at the pass. Sometimes the clouds would part, revealing the vast, black cliffs that surrounded me. Only then did I see a glimpse of cracked, vertical rock, with the snow sticking to it like paste and freezing to the stone, forming a network of white ice across it. On down. I felt like I was in the Arctic, with nothing but shawdowy shapes of overhanging mountains, gray clouds, and white driving snow. Then a shot rang out. A huge eight-point buck. All that bone and muscle rocketed away in front of me down the slope, its hooves cracking on the heaps of black rock like gunfire. Then the clouds swallowed it. I hadn't seen it against the formless background until I had almost walked up to it.

Eventually I came upon another alpine meadow with no trees, so I crouched down beside some boulders and a bush, pulled my tarp over myself, and ate lunch. It was pleasant there, with the snow tapping like a typewriter on the tarp, but eventually my feet became numb and my ankles cramped. An inch or so of snow had collected on the tarp, and now the meadow was a lake of white, with several humps where previously rocks had been.

My descent was pleasant, for I knew I was walking away from the harshest part, and I felt warm inside my several layers of clothes. I'd slip at some sections and would come reeling back to land on my buttocks and sleeping bag, and then I'd follow with the usual choice words that habit forced out, but also with a laugh. I wished I had someone to take my picture. I could feel that snow had piled up on my head and pack, become encrusted in my beard and moustache, and caked my boots. I had to kick my boots against a rock, as snow would pack under the soles until I almost had platforms of ice.

But the descent was long, and I sang Christmas carols as I entered the forest again with aching feet and shoulders. I want to go home; I itch so much to get out of here, to let my parents know I'm all right. These passes play with me; I'm only twenty miles from Forrester Pass, the most southerly one in the High Sierra, but the snow has come. I'm excited about my close proximity to the end but frustrated by the conditions. Longing to get out of here sits like a shot put in my chest.

I rushed to collect firewood. My hands were too numb to hold a match stick long enough for some paper scraps to catch fire, but then I burned my fingers in striking a match and accidently dropped it into the wood. A wisp of smoke arose, one or two sparks sputtered, and the fire began. My water bottles had shrunk from the cold, and in tromping from a stream I spilled half a bottle on myself. It froze quickly.

I don't think I've ever eaten so fast — a whole pot of rice, green beans from Lee Vining, and margarine from the bearded ranger. I lay out my tarp and rolled up in it with my sleeping bag and all my clothes on. Snow keeps coming.

October 15

Apparently the snow stopped falling sometime during the night, because it wasn't quite as high as I had thought it would be, even though now it was snowing hard and piling up on me.

I slept with boots in my bag and slept fairly well, but I decided to detour. I kept feeling it'd be wonderful to say I'd gotten through, and I only had one major High Sierra pass left. But when I thought of what I was really risking — with the chance of more snow, food low, and no tent — I decided to take a side trail which, in fourteen miles, led to a road. I was passing up being able to see Mount Whitney, which hurt an awful lot. A fresh onslaught of snow reassured me that my decision was probably the best. Thick clouds came from behind and below, up the canyon.

The trail was long; I kept descending down one canyon which would feed into another, then into another, on and on down. The trees became thicker and the snow a little less. I skipped lunch, for it was a little too chilly to stay.

After eight miles I met a couple, Jim and Sue Higman, who

offered me a campsite next to theirs. I had wanted to press on six more miles, but the thought of company was appealing.

A new heavy snow began falling, but the three of us talked around it, while another hiker joined us for a while. Sue and the other hiker eventually went to sleep, and Jim and I talked for a while longer, but then we stopped and listened to the snowflakes hiss as they touched the fire.

October 16

The sky was beginning to clear, but soon it began dumping snow again. Snow was about a foot deep now; I imagine at the passes it's about four or five feet. My boots froze last night, and the tongue on one cracked when I tried to put it on.

But Jim's and Sue's company was great; I left, planning on seeing them at the road six miles farther. After an hour of descending I left the snow, and my feet and fingers began to tingle again, then ache and burn, and then feel warm. At times the canyon opened and I could see spectacular mountains laced with snow; it was hard to believe that I was much higher than those peaks just a day ago.

The road appeared soon, with a few clean hikers standing near it. I stopped and sat by a tree and ate banana chips until Jim and Sue arrived. They gave me a ride to Cedar Grove. After consultation with Jim, who knew the area fairly well, I decided to follow the Kern Canyon to Weldon — a low steep-sided canyon. But to get to the canyon I'd have to make one more climb up over the Western Divide. At any rate, I wouldn't see the PCT for a week, and I'd have to hike with a Forest Service map that lacked contours.

Well, I missed Mt. Whitney, but I got to see the world's largest trees. Cedar Grove was located in the middle of the giant sequoias, and I had a chance to see the General Sherman Tree, the world's largest. These trees were so tall that one really can't comprehend their size by looking at them.

But here I am, in this little tourist outpost, standing in snow slush in the deepening evening. Jim and Sue had been wonderful to me, and I hated to see them go. I bought some cheese, film, and doughnuts at the store there. But I was totally without a home. The familiar PCT was now winding under the snow some miles to the east of me, by Mount Whitney, and I was here in a place without maps, in a totally foreign area. All my life when I'd seen snow before I had been home, and now I was seeing it in a civilized setting without really knowing where I was. I felt a huge hole in my chest; I wanted to be home so bad that I ached.

Faced with the prospect of sleeping somewhere in the slush, I meandered over to an empty gift shop, its lights the only ones left shining in the dark. I struck up a conversation with a small, chubby guy there about my age, and he invited me to stay with him in his one-room cabin.

The cabin had a small heater in it, but just being dry was such a joy. Before going there I had coffee with him and some trail builders at a cafe next to the gift shop, although I didn't try to strike up a conversation with any of them.

October 17

All last night the radio was on, and the unfamiliar songs of a world that was existing apart from me flooded my dreams. That world seems so distant and magical now. But the day is beautiful. The rangers here seem to know absolutely nothing about any trails here, so I could only rely on the Forest Service map as my guide. I said goodbye to the guy who had let me stay with him and started off towards Giant Forest. It took the better part of the day on roads to get there.

At Giant Forest I bought tomato juice and sweet rolls and

began to look for a warm, quiet, secluded place to eat. A bathroom next to a restaurant was a great place, and I ate in a stall there. I talked for a while with someone who was up for vacation, and he seemed to be very interested in what I was doing. I don't know what it is when I talk to someone clothed nicely, someone clean, warm, and fresh, but I feel superior or inferior or something — just very distant.

My trip over the Divide and into the Kern Canyon was going to be longer than if I hadn't detoured[38] at all, but at least in the canyon I'd be out of high country and snow. I walked up a closed road covered with snow, past groves and groves of sequoias. I was in a fairyland as the evening began to fall and the sun winked between trees, putting the forest in a dim, silver light.

The High Sierra Trail was buried under about a foot of snow as I began walking on it, and when I came to my first patch of dry ground I made camp. I was on a cliff overlooking a canyon, with the Great Western Divide standing like a wall twelve miles to my left.

October 18

My tarp crackled with ice, but the day was clear. All day I traversed a ridge, crossing patches of snow when it curved northward and walking on dry ground when it curved south. Because I had very little idea of the terrain from my map, I had no hint where water would be; so I stopped for lunch at the first stream I came to.

I began to get worried, for the trail started to wind up a gentle slope and was hard to detect under the snow. Then I noticed that fresh bear tracks, which I had seen periodically throughout the day, were still with me. Apparently that bear knew where the trail was, for I followed his tracks for a mile or two through deep snow up to an abandoned and boarded up ranger's cabin.

The Divide loomed near now, and my loneliness hung deeper as I stood on the wooden porch at this place and looked at unfamiliar mountains. I did find a good contour map, which I studied for a while, but it was taped to the inside of a window, so I had to commit to memory as many features as I could.

Off again and up a steep wall. The ridge dives off to my right, down a few hundred feet. I slipped on a patch of moss and came within a few inches of the edge.

Now deer tracks led me through snow to a campsite by a lake, the last one before the wall of the Divide. I camped on a bare snowless rock, hung my food, and made a culinary discovery with cheese and mashed potatoes. I enjoyed that dinner probably more than any other trail dinner yet. The lake was situated in a basin of rock, and the low temperatures cracked the stone and sent thundering masses of boulders crashing down to the lake all night. I was a safe distance from it all, and all night my sleep was interrupted by gunshot-like cracks of sound.

October 19

A cold, cold morning. The trail became no more than a deep groove cut into a sheer vertical wall of stone. At places where springs had crossed the way in summer, a sheet of ice now covered the ground. I inched across on my hands and knees, always conscious of the abyss on my right. One spring still spouted a rooster tail of water over the trail, but because it was lined with ice, I had to stand with the full flow of water hitting me in the legs and stomach while I searched for handholds on the opposite side; but the sun dried me out in about an hour.

The snow was a soft two feet deep, and with my dark goggles on, I walked through a white, shining boulder field under a cold yellow sun. The snow tired me out; and because I didn't know where the ridge top was, anxiety again surfaced. I had lunch on a dry boulder, but the wind was cold and I moved on. When another vast wall of mountains rose into sight, I yelled a lungful of air with all the volume I could muster, and then I found I didn't have to climb it; I was only a hundred feet from the top of the Divide.

Down the other side I hastened to Big Arroyo, the stream I'd be following to the Kern River. And the knowledge that that had been my last High Sierra climb made me almost bounce when I walked. I made fairly good time down to where there were trees; then the trail became steep again, and I camped under a full moon by the crashing stream. One more full moon. My next one will be shining on me and the Mexican border, hopefully.

October 20

The hike today was made quite exciting by the trail crossing Big Arroyo five or six times. I got pretty good at just sprinting right across over boulders. At times, though, I began to lose the trail in the marshy meadows lining the river. Upon one crossing I became royally lost. The trail was nowhere to be found, and for the better part of the afternoon I pushed through manzanita bushes until I resigned myself to retracing my steps until I found it back at the river.

For lunch I read quite a bit of Dostoevsky; I hadn't picked it up for days. And from a ridge later in the day I had a good vantage point to get my very last glimpse of high mountains. The High Sierra sat like a line of pyramids, creamy white in the sinking sun. The PCT was over there somewhere, but I'd never be there again.

A steep, knee-knocking and foot-aching descent brought me on down to seven thousand feet and the Kern River, a sinuous ribbon winding at the floor of a canyon with thousand-foot walls. It looked so inviting. I camped soon, overjoyed by the abundance of water, wood, and warm air. The night turned cold, but I felt very comfortable and kept my fire going for quite a while.

October 21

The day's hike was easy and uneventful. I'm crossing high brown grass again, though, so the terrain is making a distinct change. I paused at another unmanned ranger cabin to search for water, and then moved on past duck dotted lakes, walking along a pine needle strewn trail. The sky is very clear. I stopped to scratch my feet at a stream, and the trilling of crickets enveloped me. I'm definitely at lower altitudes.

At one clearing I stopped for lunch, sitting on a log among oak and maple leaves. The hardwoods gave me memories of the east, and I was calm and moved enough to pull out my pencil and write:

"I just had to note how beautiful it is to be out of the high mountains. I had lunch today in a grove of hardwoods. The crisp wind and dry leaves remind me so much of home that I don't want to hike. It's been a tiring ritual today; but it's incredibly gorgeous here. The air of Halloween, or the feeling of that time of year, is everywhere."

> *Tonight is one of those times when I*
> *would like to be suddenly transplanted*
> *back into my home. — I can fit myself so*
> *vividly into the very day, hour, and*
> *minute of the life and details that always*
> *take place at just this time of year.*
>
> N.C. Wyeth, **The Wyeths**

I passed a few campers as dark grew on, and I knew I was approaching a road. Most of them were fishermen who just nodded as I passed. I climbed away from the Kern, said goodbye to it, and marched down a sloping meadow to a water source, right next to the camp of about ten men and their twelve horses. They were pretty burly and not very friendly, so I didn't say much, but I camped by a tree downhill from them, where I made a meal of tuna, cheese, and noodles. At least I gave them a good show by catching my stove on fire and tossing it around to put out the flame.

October 22, 23

I was off by the time the cowboys above me on the slope were frying up some ham and eggs. The grass was crunchy with frost, but the sun was going to be hot. Because I began to see more and more hikers, I knew I was nearing a road, and so without guilt I dug into my supply of peanut butter and honey. After a steep descent I came to a paved road. It's hard to explain my excitement of nearing Weldon. That food drop has always held a magical sound whenever anyone has said it, for it meant the end of the High Sierra and the beginning of the last stretch of trail. I can't believe I'm almost there, especially since the storm threat has shadowed me daily, and since I have not called home for three weeks.

Tom passed through Isabella as he neared Weldon, meeting ". . . an old, wheezing, but active Chinese man and his tall, quiet, good old boy type partner . . ." outside Isabella. One or more pages of the journal are missing, and Tom fills in with the following recollection:

> The two men had a car parked on the road, and we had a Coca-Cola together while they set out lawn chairs and relaxed. I left them and walked about twenty-five miles along a road that provided a straight shot out of the Kern valley. I missed the Dome Land Wilderness (I guess I was about three thousand feet below it).

> I spent that night in a little town called Isabella just north of the lake by that name. The town park provided smooth grass to sleep on and public bathrooms nearby, although sleeping in the middle of a town did not put me at ease.

Probably the most memorable event while I stayed there was meeting someone in the public restroom the next morning. He was an old, grizzled man who had spent the entire night there, burning bathroom tissue to stay warm. He said that he had just beaten his wife and was "hanging out" until daylight. I got out of there and began walking towards Weldon.

There were two memorable things about Weldon. One was the postmistress named Rose, who was diametrically opposite in character from the old man. She gave me my food box and a cup of coffee, and we talked for a good while as I packed and she distributed the mail. The other event was lunch. Next door was an elementary school, the only other building in Weldon. I asked one of the cooks in the cafeteria if I could have lunch there. She agreed, but only if I sat at the far table, away from the children. I must have been pretty aromatic. Some kids gathered around anyway and told me how I could dig trenches in the Mojave and cover myself with sagebrush to keep warm. I spent the rest of the day at the post office, trying to call home and writing letters.

Penny and Bill have not come yet. I don't understand. I would have thought they'd have passed by here already. Rose dropped me off by a grocery store a mile down the road. Her name best describes what that lady was like.

I ate a box of doughnuts and drank a quart of milk at the store and then began a two mile walk down the road to a KOA Campground, where I luxuriated in my first shower in over a month. A check in the mirror there showed tanned arms, legs, and face, and the whiteness of my torso made it seem all the more emaciated. The climax of the day was the ensuing call home. No one there.

October 24, 25

I called home and finally got an answer. Mom and Dad told me they have a ticket waiting for a November 17 flight. I hope I get there by then. With clean clothes and scrubbed skin I left Weldon, with no word from Penny and Bill. The next thirty miles of trail was along paved road weaving through the brown Tehachapi Mountains. Since I could ride and still stay on the trail, I accepted a couple of rides offered to me. Four guys were tossing down cans and cans of beer in a huge old black and run-down station wagon, and they gave me a ride for a while.

My first water source was dry. A sandy gully nestled in a bunch of chaparral was all there was. Finally I found a spigot spewing water in a trough which had DON'T DRINK, WORMS carved on it. I filled up anyway and walked on up the road to the crest of the Tehachapis where nothing taller than my head grew if anything grew at all.

The sun disappeared as I descended the other side, and the temperature dropped. A pack of coyotes surrounded me, for in the grass and brush I could hear their mournful high-pitched cackling and yelping. Then I realized I was lost. I stood there pondering maps when two pinpoints of light slid over the mountains about five miles ahead. Eventually the van pulled up beside me, and a woman stuck her head out and said, "We're lost."

Again, a page is missing, and Tom fills in the gap:

> I wasn't much help, but they took me into their warm van, and together with their road map and my contour maps, we figured out where we were. They gave me a ride up the hill, out of the canyon and back to where I had gotten lost, and they drove off back towards the desert.
>
> I slept among some creosote bushes that night and

began the next day by walking out of the Tehachipis and into the Mojave. The temperature dropped and the wind picked up, so I had on wool pants and a sweater. The metal lids covering the L.A. Aqueduct, which the trail follows for a good forty to forty-five miles, were sealed shut. They're spaced four miles apart on that segment, and the first few were impossible to open.

The land was so flat and barren that I could read and walk at the same time. During lunch a green pickup drove by, and Mr. Allen, the aqueduct caretaker, invited me out of the wind and into his truck to talk for a while. He was very kind, and we talked for some time until I got the urge to move on. He told me about other hikers who had come through here and kept saying he wished I could've stopped by his house for a rest. Man, I wished I had, too, if only I'd known where he lived.

The march continued, and soon I found a cover I could remove to gain access to the Los Angeles Aqueduct. Water rushed far below, but my arm couldn't reach it. Four miles further I found another one and could reach down with my water bottle, being careful not to let the rushing water whisk it out of my hand. What a great supply, and in the desert of all places!

Darkness fell, but I easily kept walking. The wind was high, and in the distance a train was howling. It shrieked by when I got to the tracks, and the pitch of its roar plunged as it passed by. A cluster of about four Joshua trees was all the wind break I could find, but they were so unmoving and solid that the wind merely whistled loudly and seemed to almost shake the ground. I camped here with a cold dinner.

October 26

Last night my pack toppled over on me and woke me up, the wind howling like a banshee. A little rain spluttered, and when

I pulled my tarp around me, a sleeping pad darted away, carried by the wind. I cried with dismay but saw a bush catch it. I wasn't about to try to get out of my bag to retrieve it. Some little warm furry thing, I don't know what, tried to scratch in by my shoulder, into my sleeping bag, but I brushed him away. I guess I'm the only warm thing around here.

I hurried through breakfast as fast as I could. The wind is incredible. It's as if gravity became inverted to the horizon. I had to walk with head down and knees bent to keep my balance. There was a large, flat, solid cloud cover trying to push over the Tehachapis on my right, but the clouds were dissipating as they reached the desert's edge. Joshua trees are prevalent now, head-high, scaley, and contorted. They shriek and howl with the wind slipping through.

A clump of mountains lay about ten miles to the south, standing like a shrine in the middle of the desert floor, and all day long it slowly revolved as I walked by it. But the wind won't stop. My right hand and face are numb from the cold. I sat down behind a low bank of earth to stop and eat lunch; when I again stood up I was almost bowled right over. I imagined myself looking like a sped-up film of a drunkard staggering down a sidewalk. Towards afternoon the wind began to die, though, and I read my book, still marching over completely flat ground. I can see a jack rabbit flicker from bush to bush every once in a while.

Once I heard a popping sound to my right, followed by a buzzing whiz closer by. By the time it had stopped I realized someone had been shooting at me or near me.

The sun set, the wind picked up, and it became cold again. I pulled out my harmonica and wheezed away as I walked into darkness. A distant house stood solid and homey, with a warm light coming from inside it, and I had an awful urge to walk over to it, but I kept on going.

"I had to walk with head down and knees bent to keep my balance."

I found a depression like a ditch and made camp there. The wind sounded like WWII, but I was relatively protected. The thought of a waiting plane ticket kept me going today. I want more than anything else to be finished. It's only about three weeks away, but I've been counting days for so long that it still seems far away. Unapproachably far. But I get so completely down on myself that I hate this.

October 27

The day is clear and the wind not very strong. After a few miles I met a myriad of old dirt roads striking south, and after much deliberation I decided on one. Because I was leaving my water supply for good, I stocked up once more at the aqueduct, at an access place where a coffee can with a string tied onto it sat by the cover.

I could see the entire day's hike lying ahead of me: a brown line pointing across fifteen miles of desert to the distant haze of the Sierra Pelona highlands at the southern end. I read all day during that long plod, promising myself a rest every three miles. I stripped to shorts and T-shirt, although the day didn't get too hot.

A few patches of onion fields surrounded me, with one house to the east, and I met an old farmer and talked with him for awhile. Then later Mr. Allen drove up. The dirt road had become paved, so he could travel fairly easily on it.

At the southern end of the desert, brown grass grew profusely, and the sun setting behind my back put everything in a golden haze. A flock of sheep the color of the grass grazed to my left, with a Mexican-looking shepherd standing amongst them. He eyed me as I passed.

I had drunk my water hours ago, and so the thought of reaching the Fairmont Reservoir before camp whetted my motivation. After climbing over a barbed wire fence I came to the reservoir which was about the size of a football field and surrounded by bright lights. It was sunk into the ground with concrete sides, so about the only way to get water would be to dive in. The caretaker's house was over to the side. It was very dark now, and I had to steel myself before going up to his house. A potbellied man in undershirt, pants, and socks told me where a spigot was, and then he closed the door. After filling up, I walked around the reservoir, which looked so strange sitting here like a helicopter landing platform. Under the glow of an isolated streetlight, I changed back into warm clothes while an unseen dog growled from the dark. He left when I started walking again. It's so quiet now. I climbed up a dirt road, up into the foothills of this next range of mountains, and made camp on a grassy ledge overlooking the desert. The stars are beautiful, and I watched silent airplanes twinkling as they floated by until I fell asleep.

Today I had one of my best and one of my worst experiences. There's a tiny community named Lake Hughes on the San Andreas Fault a few miles south of me on the trail. When I went tromping through, a thin, prematurely wrinkled dark-haired woman invited me into her two-room home for some coffee. She loved hikers, took them in as her own children, and the coffee grew into bacon, eggs, and pancakes. She was always trembling a little as if she were nervous. She was apologetic, but we had a wonderful talk. She works as a welder in the town since her husband had hurt his back. I wondered if he was a shepherd, because she kept saying in reference to her home, "Oh, this is just an old shepherd's shack." After an hour of complete release from the trail, I thanked her profusely, promising to write when I finished, and she hugged me goodbye. For a few minutes I perused a small, nearby store, then I struck off again, searching for the trail on the slopes of the chaparral choked ridge. But what a wonderful person; I'll never forget her.

I could see the dirt road which constituted the trail up above me, so I decided to take a shortcut up through the bushes. They were like barbed wire. For two hours I whacked and pushed through that stuff, at first cursing and mumbling, then yelling, and finally giving way to tears, until I came out onto the road bleeding, sweating, and panting. Then I realized the brambles had snatched my sleeping pads and sweater. I found the pads, but my sweater is lost in the chapparal of the Sierra Pelonas.

I didn't get much further. I followed that road the rest of the day, with periodic glances back into the Mojave, until I crossed a few ridges and descended to another road with a ranger station by it. There a bundled up man gave me water from a spigot. It began to get dark, and this was my only water supply for miles, so I camped in a small park by a NO OVERNIGHT CAMPING sign.

October 29

Two months ago I celebrated my birthday. The air was very cold, and the thought of waking up in a warm bed at home made my heart tighten with excitement. Yet the miles to go are such a barrier. I can't describe what an unattainable heaven home seems to me now.

I restocked with water and climbed up the next ridge. All day the trail just dipped and wove through gullies and ridges, over land that sported nothing but chaparral and stubby oaks. The lack of water sent me panting, and I stripped to shorts and T-shirt.

A man with a rifle stood on the ridge above me. Then I saw a woman next to him, and he looked at my legs white with scratches and said, "That chaparral's pretty mean stuff, isn't it?" I nodded and we talked a moment. He had been deer hunting.

Before they left via a dirt road nearby, he gave me a couple of cups of water, most of which I downed right there. I descended the canyon of scrubby bushes, and upon walking up the other side I could see the trail distinctly weaving down the side I had just come. Big Oak Spring sported big oaks but no spring, and after a forty-five minute absence from the trail searching for it, I walked over the last Sierra Pelona ridge, where winds reminiscent of the Mojave whipped around me. The sun was almost gone, and after a few miles under a starry sky I made camp right on the trail with no water. The wind was still strong and cold, and a few of those little fuzzy warm critters again tried to push into my sleeping bag with me. The lights of Acton twinkled in the valley below.

October 30, 31

The wind is still very strong, and I made good time traversing these ridges. I tried to get a picture of the San Gabriel Mountains, but I couldn't keep steady; the wind knocked me over. A black raven floated above me, having the best time. He was a few feet above me, flapping his wings like crazy, and yet the wind kept him suspended right there. He even turned upside down with his beak open, like he was on a roller coaster, but he knew what he was doing, for he could work his way upwind eventually.

The trail, however, stopped. I followed a road, ending up on the wrong side of a fence marked NO TRESPASSING. Lucky it was early in the morning. But a pack of dogs came skidding around a barn, baying like their tails were on fire, but they never got too close, just escorted me past a few farm buildings to the road I was trying to reach.

Acton was at the end of eight miles of paved road. I did meet someone who showed me a house where I could get water from a spigot, and then upon entering Acton I guzzled apple juice and had some ice cream at the one store there. I watched the P.O. and wished I had a box coming in.

One or more pages are missing, and Tom furnishes the following:

My maps showed that the trail followed by a paved road all the way to Wrightwood, and with the pressure of making time upon me, I decided to walk the road which parelleled the trail. The grade was much easier and the distance shorter, although the walk was very boring. Paved roads aren't the same as the trail.

I met a middled-aged man and struck up a conversation with him. He was very amiable and talkative, and since he was traveling through also, we decided to make camp off the road. I was full of dinner and deep in my sleeping bag when he began propositioning me. I wasn't used to something like this, and in fact I've never — at least to my knowledge — met a homosexual before. So, being short on words and him being big in build and standing next to me, I sat up and pulled out my knife.

I'm being too dramatic here: I don't think he even saw the knife, and I certainly wasn't threatening. I began putting on my boots and packing up. The man was really a pitiful sight. He told me he understood why I was leaving and he said goodbye.

I knew the hike would have bad experiences, but I expected them to at least be ones I'd want to tell people about. I guess that's why I had such a bad feeling about this. It was a big black blotch on that segment of the hike. Although nothing happened, the thought still made me angry and despondent. I hiked about three or four more miles in pitch black that night, mostly out of a slight fear he might be following me.

The next morning, after a night spent in a ravine hidden off the beaten path, I came back to the road and walked on towards Wrightwood. I caught a ride the last miles into town.

That was when my food box hadn't arrived, and I met the wonderful Le Fevres. They took me in and let me help out with the chores. It was there that I met the bicycler, whom they had taken in for a few weeks. He and I talked for a while and then went to a sandwich shop for lunch, since neither of us had any appetizing food. That's when I noticed all the people dressed up for Halloween.

He and I were having lunch together when it suddenly hit me that it was Halloween; all the waitresses and almost everyone in the town had dressed up in costumes. I didn't stand out until I snatched a half-eaten sandwich that the waitress was going to throw away from a vacant table.

He and I shared some unusual traits, both of us, for example, being very careful with our food. Although his companionship was a joy to me, and maybe mine to him, when we shared food we always kept a watchful eye on how much each other took; he had my milk and I had his cereal. But there was a bond there, an inexpressible bond of wayfarers. I felt very close to him.

November 1

The box didn't come yesterday, nor today. I was in a real bind, the first time I'd arrived ahead of my food box. Looks like the market here will have to see me through. I decided to take the day off to prepare for the next two-week segment of the trail and to rest up a bit.

The LeFevres treated me to a dinner at a new restaurant, and after a large salad we talked for a while before crawling under sheets on mattresses laid on the floor. A stereo hummed dreamily all night long. This taste of home made my insides tighten so much I thought I would explode. In two weeks ... just two weeks ... I'll be home. God, I can't believe it!

November 2

My food box still hasn't come. I asked the postmaster to forward it when it came to Warner Springs, a little outpost sixty miles from the border. At 3:00 P.M. that afternoon I was well-stocked, washed clean, and had helped the LeFevres some more in moving some stuff. With many goodbyes, I struck off.

I had to walk through a few backyards with a dog gnawing at my heels before I came to a paved road which would take me to the trail. I came upon I-15, a roaring and rushing torrent of cars. I crossed by a bridge and a few miles farther found the trail.

It was now completely dark, and walking by flashlight was sure to get me lost, so I bedded down almost out of earshot from the highway. Although it's chilly out, a mosquito whined right above my ear, so I crawled deep into the bag.

November 3

I tried awfully hard to find the trail, but the soil is so rotten it caves in at every step. I had no idea what I was following, if anything at all. The ground is void of vegetation except for sparsely spaced squat bushes, so almost anything looks like the trail.

I decided to take another road hike, which would put me in good standing distance-wise. I made excellent time on the flat paved road and even filled my water bottles at a store. It's quite warm now, and I sweated away until I stopped for lunch under a cool oak tree.

The hike was long and tiring and very hot as I climbed up to a plateau overlooking the Mojave to the north. A vast, empty reservoir lay spread out almost to the horizon, and now it's a nest of dirt-bikers and ORVs. My last water source for twenty miles was a long, deep, cool concrete canal swollen with crystal clear water sliding down to a small reservoir to the south. It also had a large fence around it, and I scrambled over it. After savoring the feeling of weightlessness while not having my pack on, and the cool breeze on my sweaty back — which is smothered by the pack — I hoisted it up again and walked some more.

The hike ended at the bottom of a spillway of a dam which overlooked this huge, empty bowl. The dam seemed naked and squat with no water to press against it. A small, amoeba-infested stream rolled by here, and I camped on its sandy shores. The wind picked up quite a bit.

November 4

I noticed that my thermal blanket's missing. I saw it about a quarter mile down the creek, and after a teeth-gritting wade through the razor cold water, I retrieved it. It felt good to stand out of the water and experience the tingling rush of new life return to my feet.

A long, long uphill hike ensued. Lunch was eaten by an unexpected clear stream, among a grove of pinion oaks, but the rest of the day was a long, slow tromp up Deep Creek under a steaming hot sun and with little vegetation.

Night folded in. The sparse lights of Lake Arrowhead winked at me for a moment before I rounded a ridge, and then everything became black; a flashlight walk to my next water source. I followed the circle of light bouncing ahead of me, and the chill of the night slowly and softly began to ice my arms and legs. I had no trouble finding water as the rush of a stream sounded from the valley below, and in ten minutes I was buried in my sleeping bag with my head against a tree after a dinner of German potato salad.

November 5

I got a very early start this morning, walking as the sun glowed through the trees, not much above the horizon. Good thing I did, because I got more lost today than I ever have before. I walked right off all my maps, and so I just began to follow an old dirt road for a while. After several miles I came to a small ranger station. A man there directed me through a maze of roads, back to where I could pick up the trail.

Big Bear City was my goal for the day, a small resort community nestled around Big Bear Lake. Its lights twinkled below me as night began to dim the sky. Snow-dusted San Gorgonio Mountain lay to the southwest.

I walked on into the night, while my flashlight became dimmer and dimmer. Every hollow and gully had its own microclimate, so at times I walked into a crouching mass of chill air and other times felt a warm breeze. My flashlight blinked out, and a few miles later I stumbled onto the dirt road that led down into the village. I camped off the road in a bed of pine straw, saving the town for morning.

November 6

It was very unusual to be walking quaint, shaded streets lined with green manicured lawns and nice houses while I was still in grubby baggy clothes and backpack. Several dogs noticed me, and I usually had a few growling at me or barking while running next to me.

After cleaning my pack and throwing away trash, I went to a small store and ate my traditional civilized pig-out breakfast of banana and peach, a box of doughnuts, and a quart of milk. At a newspaper stand I learned Reagan beat Carter in the presidental election.

I found, after some map scrutiny, that if I walked about seven miles of road, I could meet the trail and save about six miles. So off I went up the road, my stomach gorged with food and sticking out over my hip belt. The familiar foot, hip, and shoulder aches began to work their way in. These road walks make me feel like I'm caught on an eternal treadmill with home as far away as ever, because I'm still walking, just as I've been walking for the past five months.

The uneasiness of not being on the trail but on a road where cars are supposed to be made it quite a relief to reach the trail. I only made a few miles before darkness and chill brought me to a gradual halt, and I rolled out the bag and cooked supper in bed. A few dogs barked around me; I hoped they wouldn't try to take any food.

> *Think of a man — he may be a genius of*
> *some kind — being confined to a highway*

> *and a park for his world to range in! I*
> *should die from mere nervousness at the*
> *thought of such confinement. I would*
> *hesitate before I were born, if those terms*
> *could be made known to me beforehand.*
>
> Henry David Thoreau
> **The Journal of Henry D. Thoreau**

November 7

Another tiring walk today. I don't want to hike. I'm counting the days — only eight more to go. Back in September I thought I'd be ecstatic by now, but I'm not at all. Eight days seems like five months when I still have 160 miles to go.

The trail was quite confusing, and San Gorgonio mountain rose like another world to the south. Mt. San Jacinto was wrapped in a heavy haze, and all the valleys below were hidden in haze. I'll be there tomorrow.

I've come to a water source, and the trail now is horribly tortuous. The ground is so loose that all the ridges are small and extremely steep, and huge washouts are numerous. I passed up a nice campsite to make more miles, and darkness halted me at Forks Springs, the source of Mission Creek. The creekbed was a large, sandy swath with just this trickle from a spring worming down the middle of it. I camped in the sand. As I tried to sleep, I began to hear voices. They seemed so real, I could tell the age and sex of the two speakers, and yet I could not make out what they were saying. I almost got up to look for them, and with this eerie backdrop of imagined sound I went to sleep.

November 8

Today was, I think, the worst day so far on the hike. I've never worked so hard to get so little distance before, except maybe in the snow of the Cascades.

I got an early start, and the bushes that were a confusing black maze last night were now an easy obstacle. But the soil was so rotten that the trail was completely washed away. I knew the direction I wanted to take, and that was downstream, but the terrain was either a shambles of boulders or steep canyon walls, a Death Valley scene. I climbed over numerous ridges that were off the trail, and ended up climbing down water spillways through branches, but always I ended up back at some little ribbon supposedly marking a trail. After several miles of this, my boots had been soaked and dried out over and over and were filled with sand. I longed for a solid, flat spot to take a step. On and on over this stuff I went, sometimes sloshing over creeks, other times climbing through branches when the ground was impassable, and sometimes crawling up ridges or boulder piles. The river changed direction each year, and so each year the terrain changed drastically. This was a great opportunity to work on path-finding, so I enjoyed a few miles of it.

Finally, in the early afternoon, I came to a flat pathway which took me up out of this canyon, and I sat down for a needed lunch, an enjoyable moment of reading, and a foot drying.

Too soon I was back on my feet, now climbing over a ridge to see a hazy view of San Gorgonio Pass and Mt. San Jacinto, all washed in a dull yellow sunlight. Then the trail disappeared again. I was hoping to get to Whitewater Canyon Road by nightfall; I could follow that all night if I had to, and I wanted to make miles. But the trail didn't want me to get there, for a fire had turned a scrubby sparsely-bushed ridge into a black graveyard. I made a beeline for Whitewater River after yelling at my misfortune for a while. The descent was steep and knee-knocking, and the canyon floor was like a beach except very rocky. I searched for a dry way to cross the river for awhile, and then I gave up and slogged through in my boots, cursing all the way.

The night fell and my entire visible world became the orb of light cast by my flashlight, powered by batteries bought in Big

Bear. I only had three miles to get to the road, and again the trail was washed out; I was just following the maze of dry streambeds going downhill. At times I'd come to a gaping black swath of ground that my flashlight couldn't illuminate. The river was in a canyon below me now; I just stayed away from it and kept on thinking about hitting that road.

Then I was trapped. A barbed wire fence on my right, the invisible blackness of the roaring river ahead and to the left. All ground that was level was washed out. I couldn't camp here, for the ground was a watery muck in which I sank to my ankles. Rather than back up, I climbed over the fence, ripping my shirt in the process. I don't know why the fence was there, for now I faced an almost vertical ridge. It was heavily bushed with thick grass though, so I gripped the flashlight in my teeth as I climbed hand over hand, hoping to be able to traverse this ridge over the wash-out and then drop down to the road. I was on the point of hysteria, I wanted to get there so badly; I whined away as I grunted up.

Then the flashlight with new batteries dimmed away to nothing. I kept on climbing, the back of my neck tense and my jaw hurting from gritting my teeth so much in frustration. Then the slope became harrowingly steep. Although I couldn't see down, or really anywhere, the pull of gravity at my back scared me enough to give this up. But now I was too terrified to go down. With a few yells of anger I crawled over to a steep indention, like a water runoff, and wedged my pack into it; and there I sat up on top of my pack, my legs dangling over the front. In this sitting-up position I dried my eyes and squirmed into my sleeping bag. Before I went to sleep, though, I could see in the far distance a finger of light spraying the canyon walls with a dim, small circle of yellow. Some poor soul was back up there; hopefully he knew his way better than I.

November 9

A small gray tick crawled across my leg. I brushed it off, ate quickly, and then started down. The climb down was harrowing. I can't believe I had climbed up this cliff to begin with. If I could have seen where I was going, I wouldn't have. I was back at the river bed, and could see now that if I backtracked a little I could cross it. But I fell face first when a rock slipped out from under me, so that when I got to the road, I just sat and breathed heavily awhile to calm myself down.

After changing socks and clothes and strapping everything wet to my pack to dry, I walked on down the road towards San Gorgonio Pass. The pass was flat from horizon to horizon, flanked on either side by the San Bernardino and the San Jacinto mountains. Threading through this valley was a roaring Interstate 10, which the PCT followed for ten miles. After walking on it for three miles I came to a green oasis of a rest area and decided to try to get a ride for the remaining seven. I'm not skipping any trail; I'll just get there quicker. A man in a pickup agreed to drive me down the highway, and after saying thank you, I dropped off and walked into the tiny town of Cabazon. There I ate at the grocery store and oiled my now dry boots at a gas station, where I also picked up a map for the hitchhike from the Mexican border to San Diego and the airport. Then I walked down lonely, empty streets devoid of buildings, people, and vegetation as the sun dipped behind the horizon. The trail was a jeep road winding up the foothills of the San Jacintos, so I walked on as darkness settled in. Camp was very pleasant. I was crouched among tall brown grass, a thousand feet above San Gorgonio Pass, eating canned corn and tomatoes while the tiny lights of cars slowly wove through the pass. There's a brisk wind here too.

November 10

The trail gave out again. I followed a temporary trail past NO TRESPASSING signs, through barnyards, past a small pen of agitated and squealing pigs, and eventually up a steep ridge — where it stopped. I made an honest hour long effort to find a path, but when I fell into a gully and ground my knee on a boulder, I gave up. Back I went, back past the pigs, the barn, and the gate, and back to walking a dirt road around this section. An empty ghost town of a camp called Twin Pines Ranch made my lunch stop.

Several pages are missing from Tom's journal — beginning with the afternoon of November 10 and continuing until the morning of November 13, during which time he covered the distance between Twin Pines Ranch and Warner Springs, some eighty to eighty-five miles by trail but possibly only fifty by the road route he took. An airline ticket for Atlanta awaited him in San Diego, courtesy of his parents, with a departure date of November 16, which explains his decision to shortcut by road, as he now relates:

I spoke to the ranger at the Vista Grande Guard Station and heard with some foreboding that a large area near Tahquitz Peak had been wiped out by fire, also that hikers had been reporting trouble with Indians of the Cahuilla Reservation where the trail passes south of Highway 371. Because time was running short — and I still had considerable distance to cover, I decided to drop off the trail that ran along the south-west flank of Mt. San Jacinto and descend to the town of Idyllwild. The thought of milk and doughnuts helped get me up and along Fuller Ridge, from where I could gaze back to San Gorgonio Pass, now seven thousand feet below. As the night set in, layers of mist dimmed my view of the distant lights of Idyllwild, producing a dreamlike effect that was broken only by my concentration on not straying from the trail, my flashlight growing ever dimmer. A mile or so short of Idyllwild I stopped for the night at a state campground.

November 11

I got going early the next morning, walked on into town,

and from a small store purchased fruit and milk. A passing motorist gave me a ride the five miles to Highway 74, where I again began walking, now on a flat and easy road, with twelve miles to cover before intersecting Highway 371. Impressive views of Tahquitz, Apache, Spitler, and Pyramid peaks provided a pleasant distraction as I walked. I didn't want to spend the night inside the reservation, so I stopped at the border and camped in a sandy area that was protected by a few boulders and trees.

November 12, 13

The next day was good for mileage. A quart of orange juice bought in the town of Cahuilla gave me impetus, so by late afternoon I was nearing the community of Oak Grove on Highway 79 — and developing a strong dislike for asphalt. The terrain I did enjoy, because the stubby apple trees and paucity of any other growth standing more than six feet high brought back memories of all the pictures I had seen of this part of southern California. Seven miles before Warner Springs a van pulled to a stop in front of me, and the driver offered a ride, which I accepted. The post office was closed when I arrived, so I took a quick look at the hot springs for which the three-building community had been named, and then I searched for a place to sleep. I found, of all things, a clubhouse next to a one-hole golf course, devoid of any humanity, so I rolled out my bag on the porch of the shack and went to sleep to the soft hum of a nearby Coke machine. The next morning I waited for a few hours for the post office to open, and there received the package that I had missed in Wrightwood. This gave me enough supplies for the last few days.

The trail crossed a wide muddy river bed but was easy to follow for quite a ways. I faced a cross-country segment straight across

San Felipe Valley, with the silver thread of a road several miles distant and below. I read letters from home along this stretch, observed by a few motionless staring cows. Lunch reminded me that water was going to be a problem.

I finally struck a road, and after walking several miles, laughing as I read a letter, I realized I was on the wrong road. Just two roads in this vast silent valley, and I picked the wrong one. A long backtrack put me late in the day on the right track.

Night enveloped the hills as I tromped up this empty paved road. I had eaten a pound of chocolate balls Mom had put in the last food box, and now I uneasily stepped down the three-mile decline of the road. Because the trail was a road, I decided to walk well into the night to make miles while I could. The world is so empty and silent. Clouds banked up against silver-hued hills to the west but dissipated before ever making it over. I passed the two-building town of San Felipe, one of which housed a small dog that cracked the silence with its barking. After awhile I came upon a highway maintenance station, lit by a cone of light from one streetlight, the only spot of light in a universe of dark. I felt a little like a trespasser as I sneaked by a fence and filled up my water bottles at a faucet by some gas pumps.

On and on. Dim, large NO TRESPASSING signs floated on either side of me, so when my feet groaned to a halt, I made camp in the ditch by the road, a light mournful wind wisping the grass around me.

November 14

A hot sunny day, and a Mack truck blaring by woke me up and got me going. This road is so empty; only one more truck passed in the next three miles. I struck out across broad San Felipe Valley through a cow pasture and then began my climb up into the Laguna Mountains, my last mountain range. The trail was impossible to follow, and near a rusty skeleton of an old mine I found a trace that put me back on track. I was following a dirt road when a sweaty old man in a hard hat rose out of the tall grass. We said hello, and when I asked for some water, of which I had none, he invited me to lunch. He had been working on establishing his property boundaries.

He was quite a person. Never taking off his hard hat, he escorted me to two old and faded overstuffed chairs sitting in the grass under a tree — his living room. While I ate crackers and drank a quart of cool water, he sat beside me and ate dates, sipped milk,and told me his life story. With every other word an expletive, he told me about living in New York and fighting Italian boys in his gang, and how forty years ago — he was now eighty — he struck gold and has been here ever since. A small aluminum tower down the hill marked the entrance to his mine. He reverently handed me a small stone shining with gold flecks. I departed with two quarts of his water — as precious to him as to me, for he drives to San Diego every two weeks to pick up food, water, and to take a bath. There was no difference in the sixty-year gap between our births. I left feeling I had found a close friend.

I climbed out of Chariot Canyon late in the day, and the trail led me through deep brush overlooking a dry, broad hilly landscape with rolling hills on and on. Highway S1 became the next segment, and again I hoped to make miles before I slept. A spectacular, warm sunset put me in deep darkness. A chill set in. The silence of this land at night astounds me.

But this walk was an uneasy one. Every half hour or so I'd hear a faint hum, and a minute later headlights would jerk around and down a hill. With a loud roar they would then explode over the hill in front of me and career by. Because I couldn't see a driver or even a car, the lights became frightening — the only thing visible of the mindless speeding monsters. One jerked into view, and suddenly the lights blinked off. They came back on as the car screamed by, but for some reason that scared me to death to hear all that noise and not be able to see a thing. I made camp a hundred yards off the road on a broad plain of mole hills. The moon showed a little of the surrounding area, and on this bumpy ground I fell asleep.

November 15

I just keep telling myself this is the next to the last day. Walking is so hard now. I can't understand it. I guess my mind realizes that I'm about to finish, so it releases my body from its grip, and I feel extremely languid. I cried that morning as I walked. My feet and hands ached from the cold, and yet I knew soon I wouldn't have to wake up like this every morning. As usual, the cry was a good release, and I felt relaxed enough to pull out the old physics book and read some as I walked. No cars, just me, the morning sun, the highway, and the hills. At the tiny resort of Mount Laguna I bought a day's supplies. When I told someone where I was headed, he offered me a ride. "We'll be there in thirty minutes," he said. I declined, of course; these last miles were mine. If I hiked no others, I had to hike these. But the thought that I'm really that close!

For some reason I'm not as excited as I thought I'd be. My emotions are draining out. I've been excited for the past month and a half, and the Whitewater and San Jacinto ordeals gave me reason to cry and yell in rage, and now I have trouble generating emotions. Also, I've been walking so long now that I really won't believe I'm through until I'm there. The next twenty-five miles might as well be six hundred, because I'm still walking.

But I've made good mileage and have worked hard, so with a slight glow inside and a little grin outside, I walked over the top of the Lagunas. The Anza-Borrego desert steamed to the east. Miles and miles of land to the horizon without a blade of grass, just brown cracked earth.

I still walked in oak trees and tall grass here, though, and the familiar ritual of weaving through some confusing dirt roads put me on the trail down Long Canyon. I wanted so badly to put myself in good standing for tomorrow, so that I could reach the border before sunset, and I pushed on into the night. The moon is bright; my last full moon.

For some reason my feet hurt terribly. I kept getting blisters where I'd never had them before. My feet seem to be giving up on me. At a dirt road I hobbled to a stop, sat in the grass, and let the tears stream. Won't it ever end? Will it ever, ever end? I kept whispering. The entire family is on my mind, and I directed my words to them. I can't wait to see you again.

The road led me to Cibbets Flat Campground, a small sectioned-off portion of grass which was heaped with campers, tents, and trailers. As I passed a ring of beer-drinking guys, one asked, "Where you hiking?"

"The border."

"Where'd you come from"

"Canada." That felt so good to say that I didn't care what their response was. One guy just said, "Damn." And after exchanging a few words, I moved on. I feel like camping alone tonight, so I decided to push on a few more miles. My feet grate in my boots painfully. I slowly approached a small rushing creek and eyed it for awhile with my flashlight. My third step missed, and I ended up sprawled in the water, my pack hanging up over my neck, pinning me up to my waist in water. With a torrent of curses I climbed out like a fat man hauling out of a bathtub.

And then it came. My spurts of tears during the morning and earlier in the night were nothing compared to this outburst. I laughed and cried bitterly at nature's last demeaning slap. For about five minutes I stared at a moon blurred by tears and pumped out every bit of pressure and frustration I could. The emotion came in waves. Someone may have· heard me gibbering, but I don't care. I then sat, sighing heavily, and decided this should be my camp. My soaked shirt draped heavily over the crook of a tree, and I ate cereal for dinner, the last dinner I have.

November 16

My shirt's frozen, but I pulled it on anyway. In the early light I could see an easier way to cross the stream, and soon I was pounding over Yellow Rose Spring. I stopped at this low shallow pass to eat a banana. My eyes followed the road down the last hill, down across Interstate 8, and up the yellow grasses of Cameron Valley. Six miles past there is Mexico; I can see the tops of a few low green hills.

My pack broke. The front zipper popped off; and I noticed my flashlight was gone. I had vainly searched for it last night, and this morning I still couldn't find it. Everything's falling apart; at least my feet feel all right. I'm not excited, not elated, just calm. A mile later at a ranger station by the highway, I checked out conditions at the border. Long, long ago in another world called Atlanta I had heard horror stories of Mexicans stealing hikers' gear and harassing them. The ranger didn't anticipate any danger, so I moved on.

The only way to cross the highway was to go under it. I climbed over a fence and headed for a drainage culvert. This was hard; I couldn't stand up, and crawling was too slow, so I duck-walked through as thumps from cars passing overhead resounded about my head. Another problem. I ended up on the wrong side of the creek. The trail followed a dirt road on the opposite side. Naturally, this one was broad and deep. After thrashing around for a while in eroded, yellow grassy pasture, I resigned myself to removing my boots and sloshing across. I resorted again to hissing, "Will this ever end?" over and over. Now I headed up Cameron Valley and stopped to eat my last lunch: apple, crackers, and peanut butter. Little things were special about that lunch: the cool lightness of taking off my pack, the taste of apple and peanut butter while just sitting by the road under a large bush, a pleasantly warm sun.

At the top of the hill — the last hill — I looked across six miles of green brush and houses to the hills of Mexico. Probably the last six miles were the last thing I wanted to do. My fatigue with hiking came in a rush, and I read pieces of my physics book as I slowly stomped out three miles of paved road. At an intersection sat Cameron Corners, a town of a few buildings. It was busy enough, though, and I ate two soft ice cream cones at a corner ice cream stand.

It was cold those last three miles. A chill wind blew strong over this flat valley, and the piercing yellow sun just hurt my eyes. I was cold. Past a few pink stucco and adobe homes with squat cacti in the front yard, and then to the empty little corner of Campo. No traffic, no people, just a border guard station and a small bar.

A young girl appeared walking across the street. She looked at me. "Where are you going?"

"The border."

"Oh. Where are you hiking from?"

"Canada.."

"Why'd you do that?" Good question. I mumbled a few things like oh, because I wanted to, it was fun, and crap like that. I just wanted to get there. But she smiled and was nice; I imagine she's seen a lot of hikers through here and understands things better than I realize.

She said she was the border guard's daughter. So I parted,

half expecting some gun-toting uniformed man trundling out after me. But all I passed was a boys' home with a group playing volleyball behind a fence. "Hey," one guy shouted, "where you headed?"

"The border," I shouted back.

That was enough for him, and he turned and continued playing. The sun sat lower and yellowed the sky as I followed a dirt road. One mile from the border I came to a fork and had to check my maps just once more. Then I came upon a dilapidated trailer home surrounded by muddy pig pens, a few rusty, wheelless cars, and two chained and frantic dogs. A long-haired guy a little younger than I was feeding the pigs.

Out of a door stepped a huge, fat black man the size of a boiler. He stomped to one of the trucks and leaned up against it. We waved. He pointed south and said, "The border's about two hundred yards that way. Where are you hiking from?" My answer produced a smile. "Well," he said, "Go on up there and come on back, and by then I'll have some spaghetti ready for you." I smiled and said, "Thank you, I'll do that," and then I walked on up. There was the border. A long and rusty barbed wire fence stood with a plastered but roofless hut behind it. I set my pack against the wooden PCT sign with THE START OF THE PCT and CANADA OR BUST written all over it, and then sat down for a while. A passerby may have thought I was about to fall asleep. I wasn't tired, just calm. I had already used up my emotions and felt like an empty vessel. Not that it was a bad feeling, just a very relaxed one. I was just happy that the day's hike was over. Washington and Oregon seem so far away — I tried hard to string it all together, to say, okay, I began in Canada, crossed three states and snow and desert and mountains and — but I couldn't do it. The day's hike is over. I smiled at the memory of the times in the first few months when I dreamed of the border, picturing myself crying with delight and dancing around. I now just sat here, slowly gazing around at the low green and brown hills. And then I performed the rituals I had planned so perfectly, grasping the barbed fence with both hands, sticking my foot and then my hand through and touching the ground, and taking a few pictures. It's over. When walking away I looked back to study the scene very hard. This was a place I never wanted to forget. I started back to the trailer, a warm feeling cradled inside.[39]

"...the day's hike was over."

Notes

Footnote number, entry date, and note.

1   June 5   Tom's home is in Atlanta, Georgia.

2   June 5   Tree frogs: Tom now suspects that the sound source was grouse.

3   June 5   Sunballs: snow that breaks loose when warmed by the sun and rolls down the slope.

4   June 5   Tree frogs: see note two.

5   June 7   Gorp: a dry mix of nuts and fruit.

6   June 8   Guidebooks: Jeffrey P. Schaffer, Ben Schifrin, Thomas Winnett, and J.C. Jenkins, *The Pacific Crest Trail*, Vol. 1 (Wilderness Press, 1977); Jeffrey P. Schaffer and Drs. Bev and Fred Hartline, *The Pacific Crest Trail*, Vol. 2 (Wilderness Press, 1979).

7   June 9   Crampons: a spiked metal plate worn over the shoe to prevent slipping.

8   June 10   Davidson College, North Carolina.

9   June 20   The farm: Home of Tom's paternal grandparents in northern Georgia.

10 July 8   28.7 trail miles skipped by Tom.

11 July 10   The prusik knot is the predecessor of today's mechanical ascender, both used as aids in ascending along a rope.

12 July 12   Suncups: the miniature valleys and ridges that appear in a mature snowfield.

13   July 14   Mrs. Hull: a college friend of Tom's mother.

14   July 14   Detour: about 125 trail miles skipped. Mt. St. Helens erupted in 1980 before Tom left Atlanta, again after he had been on the trail for one week, a third time after he had detoured. "Every trailhead leading into the Pinchot National Forest had a ranger staked out to keep hikers from entering, so we were left with little choice. As it turned out, the break was very much needed," Tom explains.

15   Aug. 21   Cheese straws: from the kitchen of Glady Marshburn, Tom's mother.

16   July 17   Frank Herbert, *Dune.*

17   Aug. 1   Paul, a brother.

18   Aug. 6   The Bells, across the street neighbors of the Marshburn family.

19   Aug. 8   Whirring: Tom's explanation for the sound ducks make in flight. Air, he believes, is being forced from their lungs by the wing action, the sound resulting as air moves through their nostrils.

20   Aug. 8   The Mojave rattler was presumably of the western diamondback species.

21   Aug. 11   Bobby, a brother.

22   Aug. 11   Eric Ryback, author of *The High Adventure of Eric Ryback* and the first person to claim he did the whole route in one continuous journey — whose claim was doubted by the authors of *The Pacific Crest Trail* (Jeffrey P. Schaffer, Ben Schifrin, Thomas Winnett, J. C. Jenkins, *The Pacific Crest Trail,* Vol. 1, Wilderness Press, 1982), p. 3.

23	Aug. 11	Margaret and Randy, a sister and her husband.
24	Aug. 18	App's: Appalachian Mountains.
25	Aug. 24	C.S. Lewis, *Mere Christianity.*
26	Aug. 31	Dempster Dumpsters: commercial rubbish bins.
27	Sept. 3	Great stories: many hikers had complained to Tom about how difficult the trail was between Mc Cloud and Burney Falls, and he regretted that he was going to miss this experience.
28	Sept. 3	About fifty-two trail miles skipped by Tom.
29	Sept. 5	Horned cows: cattle.
30	Sept. 6	Flip flops: sandals.
31	Sept. 15	About 38.5 trail miles skipped by Tom.
32	Sept. 21	Barbara and Kenny, a sister and her husband.
33	Sept. 21	Hitchhiking: Tom's detours, trail skips, and rides to and from food drop stations are noted. Except when portions of trail are skipped, rides between food drop stations and trail connections do not break the continuity of the hike.
34	Sept. 24	Dostoevsky, *Crime and Punishment.*
35	Oct. 2	Ruth, a sister; Karrie, a friend.
36	Oct. 2	Gia, Liza, and Anne: Davidson College friends.
37	Oct. 13	Taiga: evergreen forests.
38	Oct. 17	Detour: about thirteen hiking miles added.
39	Nov. 16	Back at the trailer, Tom introduced himself to John Broadnax, whom he describes as gruff but

exceedingly generous and kind. John served Tom a delicious spaghetti dinner, the two ate together, and afterwards they visited while John watched T.V. Tom slept on the ground next to the trailer that night. The next day, out of food and money, he hitchhiked to the airport, arriving at Lindberg Field three hours before his plane left for home.

Acknowledgments

Permission to use the quotations that appear in *Six-Moon Trail* has been granted from the following sources:

The Maine Woods, by Henry Thoreau (arranged with notes by Dudley C. Lunt), published by W. W. Norton & Company. Copyright 1950 by Dudley C. Lunt. Copyright renewed 1978 by Dudley C. Lunt.

The Wyeths, by N. C. Wyeth (edited by Betsy James Wyeth), published by Gambit Inc., Publishers. Copyright 1971 by Betsy James Wyeth.

The Pacific Crest Trail, Volume 2, by Jeffrey P. Schaffer, Drs. Bev and Fred Hartline, published by Wilderness Press. Copyright 1979.

The Night Country, by Loren Eiseley, published by Charles Scribner's Sons. Copyright© 1971 by Loren Eiseley.

A Thousand-Mile Walk to the Gulf, by John Muir. Copyright, 1916, by Houghton Mifflin Company. Copyright renewed 1944 by Ellen Muir Funk. Reprinted by permission of Houghton Mifflin Company.

The Journal of Henry David Thoreau by Henry David Thoreau, published by Dover Publications, Inc. Copyright 1962 by Dover Publications.

The Pacific Crest Trail Hike Planning Guide, edited by Chuck Long and published by Signpost Book Publishing. Copyright by Signpost Book Publishing.

Excerpt from *ALONE,* by Richard E. Byrd, reprinted by permission of Island Press, Star Route 1, Box 38, Covello,

California 95428, publisher of Fiftieth Anniversary Edition, 1984. Copyright 1938 by Richard E. Byrd, renewed 1966 by Marie A. Byrd.

In addition to the foregoing sources, whose cooperation in granting permission to use quotations from their publications is greatly appreciated, the publisher wishes to acknowledge the contribution of Willis Stork, Headmaster Emeritus of Polytechnic School in Pasadena, who read an early draft of the book, corrected errors and made valued suggestions. For final proofreading and editing refinements, the assistance of Janet Gray is acknowledged with appreciation.